Coastal Resilience and Climate Change: Blue Carbon, Wetlands, Estuarine Buffers, Flood Protection, Sea Level Rise, Nature-Based Solutions, Ecosystem Services

Copyright

Coastal Resilience and Climate Change: Blue Carbon, Wetlands, Estuarine Buffers, Flood Protection, Sea Level Rise, Nature-Based Solutions, Ecosystem Services

© 2025 Robert C. Brears

The author and publisher are of the same opinion regarding the views and content expressed in this work.

Disclaimer: The information in this book is provided for general knowledge and educational purposes only. While every effort has been made to ensure accuracy, the author and publisher make no representations or warranties with respect to the completeness or suitability of the content. The author and publisher accept no liability for any errors, omissions, or outcomes resulting from the application of information contained herein. Readers are advised to consult appropriate professionals or authorities before acting on any material presented.

ISBN (eBook): 978-1-991369-69-7

ISBN (Paperback): 978-1-991369-70-3

Published by Global Climate Solutions

First Edition, 2025

Cover design and interior layout by Global Climate Solutions

Table of Contents

Introduction

Coastal resilience is the ability of coastal systems—both natural and human—to recover, adapt, and thrive in the face of environmental pressures. As climate change accelerates, the importance of coastal resilience has become increasingly evident. Rising sea levels, intensifying storms, erosion, and habitat loss threaten the stability of coastal regions worldwide. These areas are home to rich ecosystems that support biodiversity and provide vital services such as carbon sequestration, storm protection, and fisheries that sustain millions of livelihoods.

Resilient coasts not only protect communities and ecosystems from immediate risks but also ensure long-term sustainability by balancing development with environmental conservation. By enhancing the natural defenses of ecosystems like mangroves, wetlands, and estuaries, coastal resilience reduces the need for costly infrastructure while promoting biodiversity. Strengthening resilience is a global priority, requiring collaboration among governments, scientists, and local communities to safeguard coastal regions for future generations.

This book explores four interconnected topics that form the foundation of coastal resilience: blue carbon ecosystems, estuarine buffers, sustainable wetlands, and technological advances. Each topic addresses a critical aspect of how coastal systems can adapt to and mitigate the impacts of climate change while maintaining ecological and human well-being.

Blue carbon ecosystems, such as mangroves, seagrass meadows, and salt marshes, are vital for their ability to sequester significant amounts of carbon while offering natural protection against storm surges and erosion. These systems serve as a crucial tool in climate mitigation but face ongoing threats from human activity and environmental change.

Estuarine systems act as natural buffers, protecting inland areas from flooding and storm damage. They also play an essential role in water filtration, biodiversity support, and nutrient cycling. Preserving and enhancing these systems is key to safeguarding their protective and ecological functions.

Sustainable wetlands highlight the delicate balance between human activities, such as agriculture and aquaculture, and environmental conservation. Developing effective strategies to ensure the sustainability of these human-sea coupled systems is essential for long-term resilience.

Technological advances, including remote sensing, AI, and engineering innovations, complement nature-based solutions by enhancing monitoring, prediction, and intervention capabilities. Together, these topics provide a comprehensive framework for resilient coastal systems.

Addressing coastal resilience requires an interdisciplinary approach that integrates science, technology, policy, and community engagement. Coastal systems are complex and interconnected, involving ecological, social, and economic dimensions that cannot be effectively addressed in isolation. Scientists provide critical insights into ecosystem functions and climate impacts, while engineers develop innovative technologies to enhance coastal defenses. Policymakers play a key role in creating frameworks that balance conservation with development, and communities bring invaluable local knowledge and active participation. By fostering collaboration across these disciplines, stakeholders can develop holistic solutions that address both immediate threats and long-term challenges, ensuring sustainable and resilient coastal systems.

This book is structured into nine chapters, each focusing on a key aspect of coastal resilience: blue carbon ecosystems, estuarine buffers, sustainable wetlands, and technological advances. The objective is to provide a comprehensive understanding of these topics, exploring their roles, challenges, and opportunities in fostering sustainable and resilient coastal systems.

Chapter 1: Foundations of Coastal Resilience

Coastal resilience refers to the ability of coastal systems—both natural and human—to adapt, recover, and thrive in response to environmental and human-induced pressures. Coastal areas are dynamic and complex, shaped by natural forces such as tides and storms, as well as human activities like development and resource use.

This chapter introduces the fundamental principles of coastal resilience, exploring the natural processes that maintain stability, such as sediment dynamics and ecosystem services. It also examines the growing challenges posed by climate change, sea-level rise, and human interference. By understanding these foundational concepts, we can better address the interconnected ecological, social, and economic dimensions of coastal resilience, laying the groundwork for sustainable solutions.

Defining Resilience in Coastal Systems

Resilience in coastal systems refers to the capacity of these environments to withstand, adapt to, and recover from disturbances, whether they are natural or human-induced. As dynamic interfaces between land and sea, coasts are shaped by complex interactions involving physical, ecological, and socio-economic processes. Understanding resilience in this context is essential for safeguarding the ecological integrity of coastal systems and the well-being of communities that depend on them.

Coastal systems are naturally dynamic, with continuous changes driven by tides, waves, currents, and sediment transport. These natural processes enable coasts to adapt to gradual environmental shifts, such as seasonal changes in weather patterns or fluctuations in sediment supply. For instance, barrier islands naturally shift and adjust in response to storm events, while mangrove forests and salt marshes absorb floodwaters, reducing the impact on inland areas. These inherent adaptive mechanisms are key elements of resilience.

However, human activities have significantly altered the natural processes that sustain coastal resilience. Urbanization, agriculture, and industrial development often lead to habitat destruction, pollution, and the disruption of sediment flows. Coastal wetlands, which provide critical ecosystem services such as water filtration and flood control, have been drained or filled for development, reducing their capacity to buffer against storm surges and rising sea levels. Overfishing, dredging, and offshore drilling further compromise the ecological balance of coastal systems. These pressures make coastal areas increasingly vulnerable to disturbances, reducing their ability to recover from events like hurricanes, tsunamis, or extreme flooding.

Resilience in coastal systems is often discussed in three key dimensions: ecological, social, and economic. Ecological resilience focuses on the capacity of natural systems to absorb disturbances while maintaining their core functions. This includes the ability of ecosystems like coral reefs and mangroves to sustain biodiversity and provide services such as wave attenuation and carbon sequestration. Social resilience, on the other hand, refers to the ability of communities to adapt to and recover from coastal hazards. Factors such as community awareness, disaster preparedness, and access to resources play a critical role in shaping social resilience. Finally, economic resilience highlights the need for adaptive economic systems that minimize financial losses and support recovery in the aftermath of coastal disasters.

Building resilience requires an integrated approach that combines these three dimensions. For example, restoring natural habitats like wetlands and mangroves enhances ecological resilience while simultaneously providing social and economic benefits, such as reducing disaster risks and supporting fisheries. Likewise, implementing adaptive policies that integrate scientific insights with community knowledge ensures that resilience efforts address local needs and priorities.

Climate change is a major driver of coastal vulnerability, making the concept of resilience even more critical. Rising sea levels, intensifying storms, and ocean acidification threaten the stability of coastal ecosystems and the communities they support. Traditional approaches to coastal management, such as hard infrastructure like seawalls, are increasingly being replaced or supplemented by nature-based solutions that work with, rather than against, natural processes. These solutions not only enhance resilience but also provide co-benefits, such as improving biodiversity and creating recreational opportunities.

The importance of resilience in coastal systems is also reflected in global frameworks like the United Nations Sustainable Development Goals (SDGs) and the Paris Agreement. These initiatives emphasize the need to strengthen the adaptive capacity of vulnerable regions, particularly coastal areas, through sustainable development, conservation, and innovation. Efforts to build resilience often involve collaboration between governments, non-governmental organizations, researchers, and local communities, recognizing that no single actor can address these challenges alone.

In addition to adaptation, resilience also encompasses the concept of recovery. Coastal systems must not only withstand disturbances but also regain their functionality after an event. For instance, a resilient mangrove forest can recover from partial damage caused by a storm, continuing to provide protection against future events. Similarly, resilient communities can rebuild infrastructure and restore livelihoods more effectively, minimizing long-term disruptions.

Ultimately, defining resilience in coastal systems is not just about bouncing back from disasters but also about thriving despite ongoing challenges. Resilience requires a proactive and forward-thinking approach that anticipates future risks and leverages opportunities for innovation and adaptation. By understanding the factors that contribute to resilience in coastal systems, we can better protect these critical environments and the people who depend on them. This foundational understanding will inform the strategies and solutions discussed in the following chapters.

Overview of Tidal Environments, Estuaries, and Wetlands

Tidal environments, estuaries, and wetlands are among the most dynamic and ecologically significant components of coastal systems. They play vital roles in maintaining biodiversity, protecting shorelines, and supporting human livelihoods. Understanding these environments is critical to appreciating their contribution to coastal resilience and addressing the challenges they face in the context of climate change and human activities.

Tidal environments are areas influenced by the regular rise and fall of sea levels caused by gravitational interactions between the Earth, moon, and sun. These areas include intertidal zones, mudflats, and tidal marshes, which serve as critical habitats for a wide range of species. The movement of tides facilitates nutrient cycling and sediment transport, supporting the productivity of these ecosystems. Tidal environments also act as natural buffers, dissipating wave energy and reducing the impact of storm surges on coastal areas. However, human activities such as coastal development and pollution have altered tidal dynamics, disrupting these essential processes.

Estuaries, the transition zones where freshwater from rivers meets saltwater from the sea, are among the most productive ecosystems on Earth. These unique environments provide habitat for diverse plant and animal species, including commercially important fish and shellfish. Estuaries are natural buffers, absorbing floodwaters and filtering pollutants before they reach open oceans. The mixing of freshwater and saltwater creates nutrient-rich conditions that support high levels of primary production, making estuaries essential for global food security. Despite their ecological importance, estuaries are under significant pressure from urbanization, agricultural runoff, and industrial pollution. These threats not only degrade the health of estuarine ecosystems but also compromise their ability to provide critical services.

Wetlands, including coastal wetlands such as mangroves, salt marshes, and seagrass beds, are vital for their role in carbon sequestration, water purification, and habitat provision. Mangroves, for example, act as natural barriers against storm surges, reducing the energy of waves and preventing coastal erosion. Salt marshes provide similar protective functions while also serving as breeding grounds for fish, birds, and other wildlife. Seagrass beds, often referred to as "blue carbon" ecosystems, store carbon in their sediments, contributing to climate change mitigation. Coastal wetlands are also important for local communities, supporting livelihoods through fisheries, tourism, and other ecosystem services. However, they are highly vulnerable to habitat destruction, pollution, and rising sea levels, which threaten their sustainability and resilience.

Together, tidal environments, estuaries, and wetlands form interconnected systems that are essential for coastal resilience. Their ecological functions contribute to the stability of coastal areas, while their ability to store carbon and regulate water cycles supports broader climate goals. These environments also provide cultural and economic value, serving as sites for recreation, education, and resource extraction. The degradation of any one component can have cascading effects on the entire coastal system, highlighting the need for integrated management approaches.

Climate change poses significant risks to these environments, including sea-level rise, increased storm intensity, and temperature changes that affect species composition and ecosystem health. Human activities, such as land reclamation and infrastructure development, further exacerbate these threats by reducing the space available for natural systems to adapt and migrate. Despite these challenges, tidal environments, estuaries, and wetlands remain critical allies in building resilient coastal systems. Their protection and restoration are central to global efforts to address the dual challenges of climate change and biodiversity loss.

In summary, tidal environments, estuaries, and wetlands are indispensable components of coastal ecosystems, providing a range of services that support resilience and sustainability. Preserving these environments is not only essential for protecting biodiversity and mitigating climate risks but also for ensuring the well-being of coastal communities worldwide. By understanding their roles and vulnerabilities, we can better implement strategies to safeguard these critical systems for future generations.

Challenges from Climate Change and Human Activity

Coastal systems face mounting challenges due to the combined impacts of climate change and human activities. These pressures threaten the resilience of coastal ecosystems and the communities that rely on them, making it critical to understand the nature and extent of these challenges to develop effective solutions.

Climate change is one of the most significant drivers of coastal degradation. Rising sea levels, caused by melting ice caps and thermal expansion of the oceans, are submerging low-lying areas, increasing the frequency and severity of flooding. This encroachment threatens habitats such as mangroves, salt marshes, and seagrass meadows, which are essential for biodiversity and coastal protection. Sea-level rise also accelerates coastal erosion, leading to the loss of beaches, cliffs, and infrastructure. These physical changes disrupt natural processes and reduce the capacity of coastal systems to adapt and recover from disturbances.

In addition to rising seas, intensifying storms and extreme weather events linked to climate change pose severe threats. Storm surges and high-energy waves associated with hurricanes and typhoons can devastate coastal communities, destroy infrastructure, and damage ecosystems. Coral reefs, which act as natural barriers against waves, are particularly vulnerable to these events. Repeated exposure to high-energy storms can weaken these ecosystems, reducing their protective functions.

Ocean warming and acidification are also altering coastal environments. Warmer sea temperatures can lead to coral bleaching, which compromises the health and biodiversity of reef ecosystems. Acidification, caused by increased carbon dioxide absorption in oceans, reduces the ability of marine organisms like shellfish and corals to build their calcium carbonate structures. This undermines their ecological roles and impacts the communities and industries that depend on them.

Human activities exacerbate these climate-related challenges by disrupting the natural balance of coastal systems. Urbanization is a major driver of habitat loss as coastal wetlands, mangroves, and estuaries are converted for residential, industrial, and recreational use. This development often involves land reclamation and the construction of hard infrastructure, such as seawalls and jetties, which can interfere with sediment transport and tidal flows, further destabilizing coastal ecosystems.

Pollution is another significant threat. Agricultural runoff containing fertilizers and pesticides leads to nutrient loading in coastal waters, causing algal blooms and hypoxic conditions that harm marine life. Industrial and urban wastewater discharges introduce toxins that accumulate in sediments and organisms, affecting the health of ecosystems and the people who rely on them for food and livelihoods. Plastic pollution, a growing global concern, also accumulates in coastal areas, disrupting habitats and endangering marine species.

Overexploitation of coastal resources, including overfishing and unsustainable aquaculture practices, places additional pressure on ecosystems. The depletion of fish stocks disrupts food webs and undermines the resilience of coastal communities that depend on fisheries for economic and food security. Unsustainable tourism, particularly in sensitive areas like coral reefs and mangroves, contributes to habitat degradation and increases pollution.

The cumulative impacts of climate change and human activity create feedback loops that exacerbate the vulnerability of coastal systems. For example, the destruction of mangroves for development reduces natural storm protection, increasing the damage caused by extreme weather events. Similarly, degraded coral reefs are less effective at buffering wave energy, leading to greater coastal erosion and flooding.

Addressing these challenges requires an integrated and collaborative approach. Protecting and restoring natural systems, such as wetlands, mangroves, and coral reefs, can enhance their resilience to climate impacts while providing essential services like carbon sequestration and storm protection. Reducing pollution through better agricultural practices, stricter waste management, and policies to address plastic waste is essential for maintaining water quality and ecosystem health. Sustainable resource management, including regulated fishing and eco-friendly tourism, can help balance human use with conservation.

In summary, the challenges posed by climate change and human activity are profound and interconnected, threatening the ecological, social, and economic stability of coastal systems. Tackling these issues requires proactive and adaptive strategies that integrate nature-based solutions, technological advancements, and collaborative governance to build resilient coastal communities and ecosystems.

Integrating Natural and Human Systems in Resilience Planning

Integrating natural and human systems in resilience planning is essential for addressing the challenges facing coastal regions. These areas are inherently dynamic, shaped by the interaction between ecological processes and human activities. Building resilience requires a holistic approach that recognizes the interconnectedness of natural ecosystems and the social and economic systems that depend on them.

Natural systems, such as mangroves, coral reefs, and wetlands, play a vital role in coastal resilience. These ecosystems provide critical services, including carbon sequestration, wave attenuation, water filtration, and biodiversity support. For instance, mangroves act as natural barriers, absorbing the energy of storm surges and reducing flooding in coastal communities. Coral reefs, similarly, protect shorelines by dissipating wave energy, while wetlands store and filter water, reducing the risk of floods and maintaining water quality. These ecological functions not only support the health of the environment but also safeguard human communities from the impacts of climate change and extreme weather events.

However, human systems often modify or degrade these natural systems, reducing their capacity to provide these essential services. Urbanization, for example, has led to the loss of wetlands and mangroves, which are frequently replaced with hard infrastructure like seawalls and levees. While such structures may offer short-term protection, they lack the adaptability of natural systems and can exacerbate erosion or alter sediment dynamics. Similarly, overfishing and unsustainable tourism can disrupt the ecological balance of coastal environments, leading to long-term degradation and reduced resilience.

To effectively integrate natural and human systems, resilience planning must focus on nature-based solutions (NBS) that leverage the adaptive capabilities of ecosystems. Restoring and conserving natural habitats, such as replanting mangroves or restoring coral reefs, not only enhances ecosystem services but also provides co-benefits for local communities. These solutions often prove more cost-effective over time compared to traditional infrastructure, as they adapt to changing environmental conditions and require less maintenance.

Community involvement is a crucial component of integrating natural and human systems. Coastal communities are often the first to experience the impacts of environmental change, and their participation in planning processes ensures that solutions are locally relevant and sustainable. Traditional ecological knowledge, which reflects generations of experience in managing coastal environments, can complement scientific insights to create strategies that balance development and conservation. For example, integrating indigenous practices for wetland management with modern restoration techniques can yield innovative solutions that address local needs.

Economic considerations must also be factored into resilience planning. Coastal areas often serve as economic hubs, supporting industries such as fisheries, tourism, and transportation. Integrating natural and human systems involves finding ways to sustain these economic activities while protecting the environment. Sustainable tourism initiatives, regulated fishing practices, and green infrastructure projects are examples of how economic development can align with ecological conservation. For instance, creating marine protected areas can enhance fish stocks, benefiting both biodiversity and local fisheries.

Policy frameworks play a key role in promoting the integration of natural and human systems. Effective governance involves coordinating efforts across multiple sectors, including environmental conservation, urban planning, and disaster management. Policies that incentivize ecosystem restoration, such as payments for ecosystem services (PES) or blue carbon credits, can encourage private sector investment in resilience projects. Additionally, regulations that limit destructive practices, such as mangrove clearing or unregulated coastal development, help protect critical ecosystems.

Integrating natural and human systems also requires adaptive management, where resilience strategies are continuously monitored, evaluated, and adjusted in response to new information and changing conditions. For example, restoring a wetland may involve ongoing monitoring to assess its effectiveness in flood mitigation and habitat provision. Adaptive management ensures that strategies remain effective over time, especially in the face of uncertain climate impacts.

In summary, the integration of natural and human systems in resilience planning is essential for creating sustainable and adaptive coastal environments. By leveraging the strengths of ecosystems, engaging communities, aligning economic activities with conservation, and implementing effective policies, resilience planning can protect both natural habitats and the people who depend on them. This holistic approach provides a pathway to addressing the complex challenges of coastal resilience in a rapidly changing world.

Chapter 2: Blue Carbon in Tidally Dominated Environments

Blue carbon ecosystems, including mangroves, salt marshes, and seagrass meadows, are critical to both climate change mitigation and coastal resilience. These ecosystems sequester significant amounts of carbon in their biomass and sediments, helping to offset greenhouse gas emissions. Beyond their carbon storage capacity, they provide essential services such as protecting shorelines from erosion, supporting biodiversity, and maintaining water quality.

Tidally dominated environments, where these ecosystems thrive, are shaped by regular tidal flows that deliver nutrients, cycle sediments, and sustain a rich diversity of life. However, these environments are under increasing pressure from human activities such as urban development, pollution, and aquaculture, as well as the impacts of climate change, including sea-level rise and warming oceans.

This chapter explores the vital role of blue carbon ecosystems in mitigating climate change and enhancing coastal resilience. It delves into the ecological processes that enable these systems to store carbon and protect coastlines, examines the threats they face, and highlights the importance of conserving and restoring these environments. By understanding the significance of blue carbon in tidally dominated ecosystems, we can better integrate them into global climate and resilience strategies for a sustainable future.

Definition and Role of Blue Carbon

Blue carbon refers to the carbon stored in coastal and marine ecosystems, specifically in habitats such as mangroves, salt marshes, and seagrass meadows. These ecosystems act as natural carbon sinks, capturing carbon dioxide from the atmosphere and storing it in their biomass and sediments over long periods. Blue carbon is distinct from terrestrial carbon because of its unique role in both mitigating climate change and supporting coastal resilience.

The primary function of blue carbon ecosystems lies in their ability to sequester and store carbon at rates far greater than terrestrial forests. For example, mangroves, salt marshes, and seagrass meadows can store carbon in their root systems and sediments for centuries or even millennia, creating long-term reservoirs of carbon. These sediments are typically low in oxygen, slowing down decomposition and enhancing carbon storage capacity. This makes blue carbon ecosystems highly effective in offsetting greenhouse gas emissions and contributing to global climate targets.

In addition to carbon sequestration, blue carbon ecosystems provide a range of ecological services critical to coastal resilience. Mangroves, for instance, act as natural barriers against storm surges, reducing wave energy and preventing coastal erosion. Salt marshes and seagrasses stabilize sediments and improve water quality by filtering pollutants and trapping excess nutrients. These ecosystems also serve as vital habitats for diverse marine and terrestrial species, supporting biodiversity and sustaining fisheries that are essential for local economies.

Blue carbon ecosystems also play a key role in mitigating the impacts of climate change. By absorbing carbon dioxide from the atmosphere, they help reduce the concentration of greenhouse gases that contribute to global warming. Moreover, their ability to buffer coastlines from extreme weather events and rising sea levels makes them indispensable for protecting vulnerable coastal communities.

Despite their importance, blue carbon ecosystems are under severe threat from human activities and environmental changes. Urban development, agriculture, and aquaculture have led to large-scale habitat destruction, reducing the extent of these ecosystems and their capacity to store carbon. Pollution from industrial and agricultural runoff further degrades these environments, impacting their ecological functions. Additionally, climate change poses significant challenges, including rising sea levels, warming waters, and ocean acidification, which can alter the structure and function of blue carbon habitats.

Protecting and restoring blue carbon ecosystems is essential for maximizing their climate and resilience benefits. Restoration initiatives, such as replanting mangroves or rehabilitating degraded salt marshes, can enhance their carbon sequestration potential and support biodiversity. Conservation policies that limit habitat destruction and regulate coastal development are equally important in preserving these critical ecosystems. International frameworks, such as the Paris Agreement, increasingly recognize the value of blue carbon and promote its inclusion in climate strategies.

In summary, blue carbon ecosystems are vital for addressing the dual challenges of climate change and coastal resilience. By capturing and storing carbon, buffering coastlines, and supporting biodiversity, they provide benefits that extend far beyond their ecological boundaries. Ensuring their protection and restoration is a key component of building a sustainable and resilient future for coastal regions and the planet.

Key Ecosystems: Mangroves, Salt Marshes, and Seagrasses

Blue carbon ecosystems, comprising mangroves, salt marshes, and seagrasses, are vital for mitigating climate change and supporting coastal resilience. Each of these ecosystems plays a distinct yet interconnected role in carbon sequestration, coastal protection, and biodiversity support. Understanding their individual contributions highlights the importance of conserving and restoring these critical habitats.

Mangroves

Mangroves are salt-tolerant trees and shrubs that grow along tropical and subtropical coastlines. These ecosystems are among the most effective carbon sinks, capable of storing large amounts of carbon in their roots, trunks, and sediments. Mangrove soils are particularly important, as they are waterlogged and low in oxygen, slowing down the decomposition of organic matter and allowing carbon to accumulate over centuries.

Beyond carbon storage, mangroves provide crucial ecosystem services. They act as natural barriers against storm surges and high waves, reducing coastal erosion and protecting inland areas from flooding. Their complex root systems trap sediments, stabilize shorelines, and maintain water quality by filtering pollutants and nutrients. Mangroves also serve as critical habitats for numerous species, including fish, crabs, and shrimp, many of which support local fisheries and global seafood markets.

However, mangroves face significant threats from human activities, including deforestation for agriculture, aquaculture, and urban development. Climate change exacerbates these pressures, with rising sea levels and changing salinity conditions threatening their long-term survival. Protecting and restoring mangroves is essential to preserving their ecological and carbon sequestration functions.

Salt Marshes

Salt marshes are coastal wetlands found in temperate and subarctic regions, dominated by salt-tolerant grasses, herbs, and shrubs. These ecosystems are highly efficient at capturing carbon, storing it in both aboveground vegetation and waterlogged sediments. Like mangroves, salt marshes slow the decomposition of organic material, allowing carbon to accumulate over long periods.

Salt marshes provide vital ecosystem services that enhance coastal resilience. They act as natural floodplains, absorbing excess water during storms and high tides, reducing the impact of flooding on coastal communities. Their vegetation traps sediments and stabilizes shorelines, preventing erosion. Salt marshes also improve water quality by filtering out pollutants and excess nutrients, reducing the risk of harmful algal blooms.

In addition to their protective functions, salt marshes support diverse wildlife, including migratory birds, shellfish, and fish. These habitats are critical for maintaining the health of coastal food webs and supporting local economies dependent on fishing and tourism. Despite their importance, salt marshes are increasingly at risk from land reclamation, pollution, and sea-level rise. Restoration efforts, such as reintroducing tidal flows and planting native vegetation, are crucial for enhancing their resilience and ecological functions.

Seagrasses

Seagrass meadows are underwater ecosystems found in shallow coastal waters worldwide. These marine plants are highly efficient at capturing and storing carbon in their leaves, roots, and sediments, earning them the title of one of the most effective blue carbon ecosystems. Seagrasses trap fine sediments and organic particles, which not only stores carbon but also improves water clarity and quality.

Seagrass meadows play a critical role in supporting marine biodiversity, serving as nurseries and habitats for numerous species, including commercially important fish, crustaceans, and sea turtles. They also provide food for species like dugongs and manatees. By stabilizing sediments, seagrasses protect coastal areas from erosion and reduce the turbidity of water, which benefits adjacent ecosystems such as coral reefs.

However, seagrasses are among the most threatened ecosystems on the planet, with global declines driven by coastal development, pollution, and mechanical damage from activities such as boating and dredging. Climate change adds further stress, as rising sea temperatures and ocean acidification impact their growth and survival. Protecting and restoring seagrass meadows is critical for maintaining their carbon storage potential and the many services they provide.

Interconnected Contributions

While each of these ecosystems—mangroves, salt marshes, and seagrasses—has unique characteristics, they often function as interconnected systems. For example, mangroves and seagrasses frequently coexist, with seagrass meadows benefiting from the sediment-trapping capabilities of mangroves. Similarly, salt marshes and seagrasses can work together to stabilize sediments and enhance water quality. Protecting one ecosystem often has cascading benefits for the others, underscoring the need for integrated conservation efforts.

Together, these blue carbon ecosystems form a critical part of the global effort to mitigate climate change and enhance coastal resilience. They provide essential services that extend far beyond carbon sequestration, from protecting shorelines and supporting biodiversity to sustaining livelihoods. However, their continued degradation highlights the urgent need for coordinated action to protect, restore, and sustainably manage these vital habitats. By investing in their preservation, we can harness their full potential to address the dual challenges of climate change and coastal vulnerability.

Carbon Sequestration Potential of Tidal Systems

Tidal systems, including mangroves, salt marshes, and seagrass meadows, are among the most effective natural carbon sinks on the planet. These ecosystems play a critical role in capturing and storing atmospheric carbon dioxide (CO_2), making them essential for mitigating climate change. Their unique environmental conditions, such as waterlogged soils and sedimentation processes, enable them to sequester carbon more efficiently than many terrestrial ecosystems.

Mechanisms of Carbon Sequestration

Tidal systems sequester carbon through both biological and physical processes. Vegetation such as mangroves, salt marsh grasses, and seagrasses absorbs CO_2 during photosynthesis, storing it in their

24

leaves, stems, and roots. Over time, as plant material decays, carbon is deposited in the soil, where waterlogged and low-oxygen conditions slow decomposition. This process prevents the release of stored carbon back into the atmosphere, enabling long-term accumulation in sediments.

Tidal systems also capture organic material transported by tides and rivers. These sediments, rich in carbon, settle in low-energy environments such as mangrove forests and salt marshes, further enhancing their sequestration capacity. This ability to trap and store carbon-rich sediments distinguishes tidal systems as exceptional carbon sinks compared to terrestrial ecosystems, where organic material is often decomposed and released more quickly.

Quantifying Carbon Storage

The carbon sequestration potential of tidal systems is remarkable. Mangroves, for example, can store up to four times more carbon per hectare than tropical rainforests. A significant portion of this carbon is stored in the soil, where it can remain for centuries or even millennia. Salt marshes and seagrass meadows also have high carbon storage capacities, with sediments often accounting for over 90% of their total carbon stocks.

Seagrasses, despite their smaller global coverage compared to mangroves and salt marshes, are highly efficient at sequestering carbon. Their root systems stabilize sediments and prevent carbon from being resuspended into the water column. Similarly, salt marshes, found in temperate regions, store large quantities of organic carbon in their soils, making them critical components of the global carbon cycle.

Factors Affecting Sequestration Potential

The carbon sequestration potential of tidal systems varies depending on several factors, including location, ecosystem health, and environmental conditions. Healthy, undisturbed ecosystems are the most effective at capturing and storing carbon. However, degraded systems lose much of this capacity and can even become sources of carbon emissions if soils are disturbed, releasing previously stored carbon.

Tidal dynamics also play a significant role in determining sequestration rates. Systems with higher sediment deposition rates, such as deltas and estuaries, often have greater carbon storage potential. Conversely, areas experiencing erosion or subsidence may lose stored carbon and reduce their overall sequestration capacity. Additionally, external pressures such as pollution, overexploitation, and land conversion significantly reduce the ability of these ecosystems to function as carbon sinks.

Climate Change and Carbon Sequestration

Climate change poses both challenges and opportunities for the carbon sequestration potential of tidal systems. Rising sea levels can submerge existing ecosystems, reducing vegetation cover and carbon storage capacity. However, if these systems are allowed to migrate inland, they may continue to accumulate carbon in new areas. Conversely, higher temperatures and ocean acidification can impair the growth of seagrasses and salt marsh plants, reducing their overall productivity and carbon uptake.

Restoration efforts, such as replanting mangroves and restoring degraded salt marshes and seagrass meadows, have demonstrated the ability to recover lost carbon sequestration capacity. These initiatives can also enhance ecosystem services, such as shoreline stabilization and biodiversity support, making them a key component of climate adaptation strategies.

Global Importance of Tidal Systems

Tidal systems represent a small fraction of the Earth's surface but play a disproportionately large role in the global carbon cycle. Their ability to store carbon long-term makes them invaluable in meeting global climate targets, such as those outlined in the Paris Agreement. Protecting and restoring these ecosystems is a cost-effective strategy for reducing greenhouse gas concentrations and mitigating climate change impacts.

In conclusion, the carbon sequestration potential of tidal systems is a critical natural solution to the climate crisis. By understanding and preserving these ecosystems, we can harness their ability to capture and store carbon while supporting broader goals of coastal resilience and biodiversity conservation.

Threats and Strategies for Protecting Blue Carbon Systems

Blue carbon systems, including mangroves, salt marshes, and seagrass meadows, play an essential role in mitigating climate change and enhancing coastal resilience. However, these ecosystems face numerous threats from human activities and environmental changes, which compromise their ability to sequester carbon and provide vital ecosystem services. Understanding these threats and implementing strategies to protect and restore blue carbon systems is critical for achieving global climate and conservation goals.

Threats to Blue Carbon Systems

1. Habitat Loss and Degradation

One of the most significant threats to blue carbon ecosystems is habitat loss due to urban development, agriculture, and aquaculture. Coastal wetlands and mangroves are often cleared for infrastructure projects or converted into farmland and shrimp farms, resulting in the destruction of these vital carbon sinks. Seagrass meadows are particularly vulnerable to mechanical damage caused by boat anchors, dredging, and coastal construction.

2. Pollution

Pollution from agricultural runoff, industrial discharges, and urban wastewater has devastating effects on blue carbon systems. Excess nutrients in coastal waters lead to eutrophication, causing algal blooms that block sunlight and reduce oxygen levels, which can kill vegetation and disrupt ecosystem functions. Plastic pollution further degrades these ecosystems by physically damaging plants and altering sediment composition.

3. Climate Change

Rising sea levels, warming ocean temperatures, and ocean acidification pose significant threats to blue carbon ecosystems. Mangroves and salt marshes struggle to adapt to rapid sea-level rise, particularly in areas where coastal development prevents their inland migration. Seagrasses, which are sensitive to temperature changes, are negatively impacted by ocean warming, leading to reduced growth and carbon sequestration capacity. Ocean acidification also affects the growth and resilience of seagrasses and other calcifying organisms within these ecosystems.

4. Overexploitation

Overfishing and unsustainable harvesting of mangrove wood and other resources weaken blue carbon systems. Depleting fish populations disrupts food webs, while cutting down mangroves for timber and fuelwood reduces their ability to store carbon and protect coastlines from storm surges and erosion.

Strategies for Protecting Blue Carbon Systems

1. Conservation and Restoration Initiatives

Protecting existing blue carbon ecosystems is the most effective way to preserve their carbon sequestration capacity. Conservation measures, such as establishing marine protected areas (MPAs), can safeguard mangroves, salt marshes, and seagrasses from harmful activities like development and overfishing. Restoration efforts, such as replanting mangroves and reintroducing tidal flows to degraded wetlands, can help recover lost carbon storage potential while enhancing biodiversity and ecosystem resilience.

2. Sustainable Coastal Development

Adopting sustainable development practices along coastlines can minimize habitat destruction. For instance, implementing zoning regulations and environmental impact assessments ensures that infrastructure projects avoid critical blue carbon areas. Green infrastructure, such as living shorelines, can replace traditional hard infrastructure, allowing natural systems to thrive while still providing coastal protection.

3. Pollution Control

Reducing pollution is essential for maintaining the health of blue carbon systems. This includes improving agricultural practices to minimize fertilizer runoff, enhancing wastewater treatment facilities, and implementing policies to curb plastic pollution. These measures help maintain water quality, which is critical for the growth and function of blue carbon ecosystems.

4. Climate Adaptation Measures

To address the impacts of climate change, strategies such as facilitating the inland migration of mangroves and salt marshes are essential. This can be achieved by designating buffer zones along coastlines where these ecosystems can expand as sea levels rise. Research and monitoring are also crucial for understanding the effects of climate change on blue carbon systems and identifying adaptive management practices.

5. Policy and Financial Incentives

International and national policies play a critical role in protecting blue carbon ecosystems. Integrating blue carbon into climate strategies, such as Nationally Determined Contributions (NDCs) under the Paris Agreement, highlights their importance in achieving climate goals. Financial incentives, such as blue carbon credits and PES, encourage stakeholders to invest in conservation and restoration efforts.

Chapter 3: Estuarine Systems as Buffers Against Climate Change

Estuarine systems, where freshwater from rivers meets saltwater from the sea, are among the most productive and dynamic ecosystems on Earth. These unique environments play a critical role in buffering coastal areas against the impacts of climate change, such as rising sea levels, intensifying storms, and flooding. By absorbing excess water, trapping sediments, and dissipating wave energy, estuaries protect both natural ecosystems and human communities.

In addition to their protective functions, estuarine systems support diverse species, serve as nurseries for commercially important fish, and provide essential ecosystem services such as water filtration and nutrient cycling. However, estuaries are increasingly under threat from human activities, including urbanization, pollution, and habitat destruction, as well as the growing pressures of climate change.

This chapter explores the vital role of estuarine systems as natural buffers against climate change. It examines the ecological processes that enable estuaries to mitigate coastal hazards, the challenges these ecosystems face, and the strategies needed to preserve and restore their functionality. Understanding the importance of estuarine systems is crucial for integrating them into broader efforts to enhance coastal resilience and support sustainable development.

Role of Estuaries as Natural Buffers

Estuaries, where freshwater from rivers merges with saltwater from the sea, are vital ecosystems that serve as natural buffers against environmental hazards. These dynamic and productive systems provide critical protection to coastal regions by mitigating the impacts of climate change, such as rising sea levels, storm surges, and coastal flooding. Their unique ecological functions, combined with their ability to support diverse habitats, make estuaries an essential component of coastal resilience.

Absorbing and Dissipating Storm Energy

One of the most important functions of estuaries is their ability to reduce the destructive energy of storms. Estuaries contain wetlands, mudflats, and tidal marshes that act as natural barriers, absorbing and dissipating the energy from waves and storm surges before they reach inland areas. These features reduce the force of storms, helping to minimize flooding and damage to infrastructure and communities. For instance, the vegetation in estuarine wetlands slows down water movement, allowing for the gradual absorption of storm surges and high tides. This buffering capacity is especially critical in regions prone to hurricanes, typhoons, and cyclones.

Trapping Sediments and Reducing Erosion

Estuarine systems play a significant role in stabilizing coastlines by trapping sediments carried by rivers and tides. The vegetation in estuarine environments, such as salt marsh grasses and mangroves, anchors sediment in place, preventing it from being washed away by waves or currents. This process reduces coastal erosion, which is a growing concern in the face of rising sea levels. By maintaining sediment balance, estuaries protect shorelines and provide a stable foundation for coastal ecosystems and human settlements.

Additionally, the sediment-trapping ability of estuaries supports the growth and persistence of critical habitats, such as tidal marshes and mudflats. These habitats not only enhance coastal resilience but also support biodiversity and provide resources for local communities, such as fisheries and tourism.

Managing Floodwaters

Estuaries act as natural floodplains, absorbing and storing excess water during periods of heavy rainfall or high river flow. This function is particularly valuable in reducing the risk of flooding in urban and agricultural areas adjacent to coastal regions. The capacity of estuarine systems to store floodwaters alleviates pressure on built infrastructure, such as levees and stormwater systems, reducing the economic and social impacts of flooding. By slowing down the flow of water, estuaries also prevent sudden surges that could otherwise overwhelm drainage systems and cause extensive damage.

Filtering Pollutants and Improving Water Quality

Estuaries function as natural filters, improving water quality by trapping sediments and absorbing pollutants before they reach open waters. Nutrients, toxins, and debris carried by rivers are intercepted by the vegetation and sediments within estuaries, reducing their impact on marine ecosystems. For example, excess nutrients from agricultural runoff, such as nitrogen and phosphorus, are absorbed by estuarine plants, preventing harmful algal blooms that can degrade water quality and harm marine life.

This water filtration capacity is particularly important for maintaining the health of downstream ecosystems, including coral reefs and seagrass beds, which are highly sensitive to pollution. By protecting water quality, estuaries support biodiversity and ensure the sustainability of fisheries and aquaculture, which many coastal communities depend on for their livelihoods.

Providing Critical Habitats

Estuaries are home to a wide range of plant and animal species, including migratory birds, fish, shellfish, and marine mammals. These ecosystems serve as breeding and nursery grounds for many commercially important species, supporting global fisheries and food security. The habitats within estuaries, such as tidal marshes and mangroves, provide shelter and resources for wildlife, contributing to the overall health and productivity of coastal ecosystems.

By maintaining biodiversity, estuaries enhance the resilience of coastal regions. Diverse ecosystems are better able to adapt to environmental changes and recover from disturbances, ensuring the continued provision of essential services.

Climate Change Mitigation

In addition to their role as buffers, estuarine systems contribute to climate change mitigation by storing carbon in their vegetation and sediments. These "blue carbon" ecosystems sequester carbon dioxide from the atmosphere, helping to reduce greenhouse gas concentrations. Mangroves and salt marshes within estuaries are particularly effective at long-term carbon storage, making them valuable tools in global climate strategies.

Mitigating Storm Surges, Flooding, and Erosion

Estuarine systems play a critical role in mitigating storm surges, flooding, and coastal erosion, making them indispensable for protecting both natural ecosystems and human communities. Their unique combination of physical, biological, and ecological functions allows estuaries to act as natural defenses, absorbing and dissipating the energy of storms and stabilizing shorelines.

Storm Surge Mitigation

Storm surges, caused by high winds and low atmospheric pressure during storms, pose a significant threat to coastal areas, often resulting in severe flooding and damage to infrastructure. Estuarine systems help reduce the impact of storm surges by acting as natural barriers that absorb and dissipate wave energy. Wetlands, mangroves, and salt marshes within estuaries provide physical resistance to incoming water, reducing its velocity and energy before it reaches inland areas. The dense vegetation in these habitats, such as the intricate root systems of mangroves or the tall grasses of salt marshes, creates friction that slows down water movement and disperses wave energy.

Tidal flats and mudflats in estuarine systems also contribute to storm surge mitigation by acting as expansive, low-lying areas that can accommodate and diffuse large volumes of water. By spreading the surge over a wider area, these features reduce the height and intensity of the waves reaching the shoreline. This natural buffering capacity protects coastal infrastructure, communities, and ecosystems from the worst impacts of storms.

Flood Mitigation

Flooding is another major challenge for coastal regions, particularly during extreme weather events or periods of heavy rainfall. Estuarine systems function as natural floodplains, absorbing excess water and preventing sudden surges that can overwhelm drainage systems. Wetlands within estuaries are especially effective in flood mitigation due to their ability to store large volumes of water in their soils and vegetation. For example, tidal wetlands act as sponges, capturing floodwaters and gradually releasing them back into the environment over time, reducing the risk of flash flooding.

In addition to reducing floodwater volume, estuarine systems also help regulate water flow. By slowing down the movement of water, they reduce the likelihood of catastrophic flooding in downstream areas. This capacity is particularly valuable in urbanized coastal regions, where hard infrastructure such as roads and buildings often prevents water from being absorbed into the ground. Estuarine systems complement built infrastructure by providing natural solutions that enhance flood resilience.

Erosion Control

Coastal erosion, driven by wave action, rising sea levels, and human activities, threatens the stability of shorelines and the infrastructure built along them. Estuarine systems play a crucial role in controlling erosion by stabilizing sediments and maintaining the integrity of coastal landscapes. Vegetation in estuarine habitats, such as salt marshes and mangroves, anchors sediment in place with their extensive root systems, reducing its susceptibility to being washed away by waves and currents.

Seagrass meadows, often found in estuarine waters, also contribute to erosion control by trapping fine sediments and reducing turbidity. These underwater plants not only stabilize the seabed but also create calmer conditions that prevent the resuspension of sediments. Together, these features help maintain the shape and stability of coastlines, reducing the need for costly interventions such as seawalls and artificial beach nourishment.

Climate Change Amplification

Climate change has intensified the risks associated with storm surges, flooding, and erosion. Rising sea levels and more frequent extreme weather events amplify these challenges, placing greater pressure on coastal regions. Estuarine systems provide a critical line of defense against these threats by offering natural, adaptive solutions. Unlike hard infrastructure, such as levees or seawalls, estuarine habitats can adjust to changing conditions, such as rising seas, by migrating inland or growing vertically through sediment accretion.

Restoration and Conservation Strategies

To enhance the capacity of estuarine systems to mitigate storm surges, flooding, and erosion, restoration and conservation efforts are essential. Restoring degraded wetlands, replanting mangroves, and protecting salt marshes can rebuild natural defenses and strengthen coastal resilience. Policies that limit coastal development in sensitive areas and promote sustainable land-use practices are also critical for maintaining the protective functions of estuarine systems.

Supporting Biodiversity and Water Quality

Estuarine systems are among the most biologically productive ecosystems on Earth, playing a vital role in supporting biodiversity and maintaining water quality. These unique environments, where freshwater meets saltwater, provide essential habitat for a wide range of species and serve as natural filters that improve water quality in coastal regions. Together, these functions contribute to the resilience and sustainability of coastal systems, benefiting both ecosystems and human communities.

Supporting Biodiversity

Estuaries provide critical habitats for diverse plant and animal species, including many that are endemic or commercially important. The dynamic mixing of freshwater and saltwater creates unique environmental conditions that support a variety of life forms adapted to these fluctuating conditions. Key habitats within estuaries, such as tidal marshes, mangroves, mudflats, and seagrass meadows, provide shelter, breeding grounds, and feeding areas for numerous species.

• **Nurseries for Marine Life**: Estuaries are often referred to as the nurseries of the sea. Many fish and shellfish species, including shrimp, crabs, and commercially valuable finfish, rely on estuarine habitats during critical stages of their life cycles. The sheltered waters and abundant food resources make estuaries ideal for juvenile species to grow and thrive before migrating to open oceans.

• **Critical Habitat for Migratory Birds**: Estuaries are vital stopover points for migratory birds along international flyways. These areas provide abundant food, such as fish, crustaceans, and invertebrates, which are essential for fueling long migrations. Birds such as herons, egrets, and sandpipers depend on estuarine ecosystems for feeding and nesting, making these areas important for global bird conservation.

• **Biodiversity Hotspots**: The diverse habitats within estuaries support rich biodiversity, from submerged aquatic vegetation and algae to mammals and reptiles. Mangroves, for example, host terrestrial and aquatic species, while mudflats support benthic organisms that form the foundation of coastal food webs.

Maintaining Water Quality

In addition to supporting biodiversity, estuarine systems play a crucial role in maintaining water quality in coastal areas. These environments act as natural filters, capturing and neutralizing pollutants, sediments, and excess nutrients before they reach open waters. This ability to improve water quality benefits both marine ecosystems and human communities.

• **Filtering Pollutants**: Estuarine vegetation, such as mangroves and salt marsh grasses, traps and stabilizes sediments that carry pollutants from upstream sources. By preventing these pollutants from entering coastal and marine ecosystems, estuaries help maintain the health of adjacent habitats, including coral reefs and seagrass beds. This function is particularly important in areas impacted by agricultural runoff and urban wastewater.

• **Absorbing Excess Nutrients**: Nutrient pollution, often caused by fertilizers and animal waste, can lead to eutrophication and harmful algal blooms. Estuaries help mitigate this issue by absorbing excess nutrients through plant uptake and microbial processes in their soils. For example, seagrass meadows and tidal marshes absorb nitrogen and phosphorus, preventing these nutrients from accumulating in coastal waters and causing ecological imbalances.

• **Reducing Sediment and Turbidity**: Sediments carried by rivers often accumulate in estuaries, where they are trapped by vegetation and deposited in mudflats and marshes. This process reduces turbidity in coastal waters, improving light penetration and benefiting habitats such as coral reefs and seagrass beds, which depend on clear water for photosynthesis.

Challenges to Biodiversity and Water Quality

Despite their importance, estuarine systems face numerous threats that compromise their ability to support biodiversity and maintain water quality. Urban development, pollution, overfishing, and climate change all place significant pressure on these ecosystems. Habitat destruction reduces the availability of critical areas for species, while pollution and nutrient runoff degrade water quality and disrupt ecological processes.

Conservation and Restoration Strategies

Protecting estuarine systems is essential for preserving their biodiversity and water quality functions. Conservation efforts, such as the establishment of marine protected areas and the enforcement of pollution controls, can safeguard these ecosystems. Restoration projects, such as replanting mangroves, restoring tidal flows, and reducing nutrient inputs, help rebuild degraded habitats and enhance their ecological functions.

Climate Change Impacts and Strategies for Resilience

Climate change poses significant challenges to estuarine systems, threatening their ecological health and ability to provide critical services such as coastal protection, biodiversity support, and water quality improvement. Rising sea levels, increasing storm intensity, warming temperatures, and ocean acidification are altering the dynamics of these ecosystems. To ensure their continued functionality and resilience, proactive strategies that address these impacts are essential.

Impacts of Climate Change on Estuarine Systems

1. **Rising Sea Levels**

Sea-level rise is one of the most visible impacts of climate change on estuaries. Higher water levels threaten to submerge tidal marshes, mudflats, and mangroves, reducing habitat availability for species that rely on these areas. When estuarine systems are unable to migrate inland due to urbanization or other barriers, their loss accelerates, leading to a decline in biodiversity and ecosystem services. Submersion of vegetation also reduces the ability of estuaries to store carbon, diminishing their role as blue carbon ecosystems.

2. **Increasing Storm Intensity**

More frequent and intense storms exacerbate erosion and damage to estuarine habitats. Storm surges can wash away vegetation, sediments, and nutrients critical for maintaining these ecosystems. Repeated exposure to such events weakens the ability of estuaries to recover, compromising their role in buffering inland areas from storm impacts.

3. **Warming Temperatures**

Rising air and water temperatures affect estuarine species and habitats in various ways. Warmer waters can lead to shifts in species composition, favoring invasive or heat-tolerant species while driving out native ones. Fish and shellfish, many of which are economically valuable, may face habitat loss or reproductive challenges due to temperature increases. Additionally, temperature stress can weaken vegetation like salt marsh grasses and mangroves, reducing their resilience to other environmental pressures.

4. **Ocean Acidification**

Increased absorption of carbon dioxide by oceans has led to acidification, which disrupts the calcification processes of marine organisms such as shellfish, crustaceans, and corals. Estuarine systems, which support these species during critical life stages, are particularly vulnerable to acidification, with cascading effects on biodiversity and food security.

5. **Altered Hydrology**

Changes in rainfall patterns and upstream water use affect the freshwater flow into estuaries. Reduced flow can increase salinity levels, stressing species adapted to specific salinity ranges. Conversely, excessive freshwater input due to extreme rainfall can disrupt the delicate balance between saltwater and freshwater, leading to habitat degradation.

Strategies for Resilience

1. Ecosystem Restoration

Restoring degraded estuarine habitats is a critical strategy for enhancing resilience. Replanting mangroves, restoring tidal flows, and rebuilding marshes can help these systems adapt to rising sea levels and increasing storm intensity. Restoration improves biodiversity, strengthens natural defenses against storms, and enhances carbon sequestration.

2. Facilitating Habitat Migration

To address the impacts of sea-level rise, it is essential to create space for estuarine systems to migrate inland. Establishing buffer zones, removing hard infrastructure where feasible, and implementing land-use policies that prioritize conservation can enable ecosystems to adapt to changing conditions.

3. Building Living Shorelines

Living shorelines, which integrate natural elements like vegetation and oyster reefs with engineering solutions, offer a hybrid approach to resilience. These systems reduce erosion, dissipate wave energy, and support biodiversity while allowing estuaries to maintain their ecological functions.

4. Water Quality Management

Enhancing water quality is critical for maintaining estuarine resilience. Reducing nutrient pollution through improved agricultural practices, controlling urban runoff, and strengthening wastewater treatment can mitigate the impacts of eutrophication and algal blooms. Healthy water conditions improve the ability of estuarine vegetation to thrive and support biodiversity.

5. Monitoring and Adaptive Management

Ongoing monitoring of estuarine systems is essential to track the impacts of climate change and evaluate the effectiveness of resilience strategies. Adaptive management, which involves adjusting practices based on new data and changing conditions, ensures that efforts remain relevant and effective over time.

6. Climate-Smart Policies

Governments play a vital role in enhancing estuarine resilience by adopting climate-smart policies. Incorporating estuarine conservation into climate action plans, providing financial incentives for restoration projects, and ensuring community participation in decision-making processes are critical for long-term resilience.

Chapter 4: Sustainability of Human-Sea Coupled Coastal Wetland Systems

Coastal wetlands, including mangroves, salt marshes, and tidal flats, represent a delicate balance between natural ecosystems and human activities. These human-sea coupled systems are critical for their ecological, economic, and cultural importance. They provide essential services such as carbon sequestration, flood control, water purification, and support for fisheries, while also serving as sites for agriculture, aquaculture, and tourism.

However, this interdependence also creates challenges. Human activities like urbanization, industrial development, and unsustainable resource extraction often degrade these ecosystems, reducing their capacity to provide benefits and threatening their long-term viability. Climate change adds further pressure, with rising sea levels, changing weather patterns, and increased storm intensity exacerbating the risks to these systems.

This chapter explores the sustainability of human-sea coupled coastal wetland systems, examining how human interactions shape these ecosystems and the strategies needed to maintain their functionality. It delves into the impacts of human activity, the ecological and social dimensions of sustainability, and the role of governance and community engagement in protecting and restoring coastal wetlands. By addressing these challenges, we can ensure that these vital ecosystems continue to support both environmental health and human livelihoods in the face of growing global pressures.

Definition and Importance of Human-Sea Coupled Systems

Human-sea coupled systems refer to the interconnected relationship between human activities and coastal marine ecosystems, where ecological processes and human livelihoods are deeply intertwined. These systems are characterized by the dynamic exchange of resources, energy, and impacts between humans and nature. In coastal wetlands, such as mangroves, salt marshes, and tidal flats, this interaction is particularly evident, as these areas provide essential ecological services while also supporting a wide range of human activities.

Definition of Human-Sea Coupled Systems

Human-sea coupled systems are defined by the reciprocal interactions between humans and the marine environment. Coastal wetlands, for example, offer crucial ecosystem services such as carbon sequestration, water purification, flood protection, and biodiversity support. At the same time, humans rely on these areas for activities such as fishing, aquaculture, agriculture, tourism, and urban development. The term "coupled" emphasizes the interdependence of these systems, where changes in one component—natural or human—inevitably affect the other.

These systems operate within a feedback loop: human activities influence the health and functionality of coastal wetlands, and in turn, the condition of these ecosystems affects the benefits and services they provide to humans. For example, overfishing can disrupt the balance of marine food webs, while degraded wetlands reduce the ability of ecosystems to buffer storm surges or filter pollutants. As such, human-sea coupled systems are complex, adaptive, and subject to both environmental and anthropogenic pressures.

Importance of Human-Sea Coupled Systems

Human-sea coupled systems are essential for both ecological health and human well-being. They play a vital role in maintaining the balance between sustainable development and environmental conservation, particularly in coastal areas where human populations are dense and natural resources are abundant.

1. Ecosystem Services

Coastal wetlands within human-sea coupled systems provide a wide range of ecosystem services that are crucial for both environmental stability and economic prosperity. These include:

• **Carbon Sequestration**: Wetlands such as mangroves and salt marshes store significant amounts of carbon, helping to mitigate climate change.

• **Flood Protection and Erosion Control**: Wetlands act as natural buffers, absorbing storm surges and stabilizing shorelines, thereby reducing the risk of flooding and erosion in coastal communities.

• **Water Purification**: Coastal wetlands filter pollutants and excess nutrients from runoff, maintaining water quality and supporting adjacent ecosystems like coral reefs and seagrass meadows.

• **Biodiversity Support**: These areas serve as habitats and nurseries for a wide range of species, including commercially valuable fish, shellfish, and migratory birds.

2. Human Livelihoods

Human-sea coupled systems are critical for the livelihoods of millions of people worldwide. Coastal communities rely on these ecosystems for food, employment, and cultural identity. Activities such as fishing, aquaculture, and ecotourism directly depend on the health and functionality of these systems. Additionally, mangrove wood and other resources from wetlands are often used for construction, fuel, and traditional practices.

3. Cultural and Social Value

Beyond their ecological and economic significance, human-sea coupled systems hold cultural, historical, and spiritual value for many communities. Coastal wetlands are often integral to local traditions, providing inspiration, recreation, and a sense of identity.

They also play a key role in education and scientific research, offering opportunities to study biodiversity and ecological processes.

4. Climate Resilience

As climate change accelerates, the importance of human-sea coupled systems in enhancing resilience becomes increasingly evident. Coastal wetlands help protect vulnerable communities from rising sea levels, extreme weather events, and other climate-related impacts. By maintaining the health of these systems, we can reduce risks to both ecosystems and human populations.

Challenges and Opportunities

The interdependence of humans and coastal wetlands also creates significant challenges. Unsustainable practices such as overfishing, pollution, and land reclamation degrade the health of these ecosystems, reducing their ability to provide critical services. Climate change further amplifies these pressures, threatening the long-term sustainability of human-sea coupled systems.

However, this interconnection also offers opportunities for mutual benefit. By adopting sustainable practices, restoring degraded ecosystems, and integrating traditional knowledge with modern science, we can enhance the resilience of these systems. Collaborative governance, community engagement, and policy support are essential for maintaining the balance between human activities and ecological health.

Human Interactions with Coastal Wetlands (Agriculture, Aquaculture, Tourism)

Coastal wetlands, including mangroves, salt marshes, and tidal flats, are dynamic ecosystems that provide essential services and resources for human activities. Over time, these wetlands have become integral to livelihoods and economies through agriculture, aquaculture, and tourism. While these interactions can create economic and social benefits, they also place significant pressures on wetland ecosystems, often leading to degradation and loss of resilience. Understanding the impacts of these interactions is essential for developing sustainable practices that balance human needs with ecological health.

Agriculture in Coastal Wetlands

Agriculture has been a prominent activity in coastal wetlands for centuries, particularly in regions where fertile soils and abundant water make these ecosystems ideal for cultivation. Crops such as rice, sugarcane, and other water-intensive plants are commonly grown in wetland areas. These agricultural practices rely on the nutrient-rich sediments deposited in wetlands, which provide natural fertility that supports high yields.

However, intensive agricultural practices in coastal wetlands can have detrimental impacts. The conversion of wetlands into farmland often involves drainage, land reclamation, and deforestation, which destroy critical habitats and reduce the capacity of wetlands to store carbon and absorb floodwaters. In addition, the use of chemical fertilizers and pesticides contributes to nutrient runoff and water pollution, leading to eutrophication in nearby aquatic systems. This degradation not only affects wetland ecosystems but also reduces the long-term viability of agricultural production in these areas.

Sustainable agricultural practices, such as agroecology and integrated water management, offer potential solutions. By adopting methods that preserve wetland functions—such as maintaining natural hydrology, minimizing chemical inputs, and rotating crops— farmers can achieve productivity while protecting the ecological integrity of coastal wetlands.

Aquaculture in Coastal Wetlands

Aquaculture, the farming of fish, shellfish, and other aquatic organisms, is a major driver of human interaction with coastal wetlands. Mangroves and salt marshes are often converted into aquaculture ponds, particularly for shrimp and fish farming. This industry has grown rapidly in response to global demand for seafood, providing income and employment to millions of people in coastal regions.

While aquaculture offers significant economic benefits, its expansion often comes at the expense of wetland ecosystems. Clearing mangroves and altering tidal flows to create ponds disrupts the natural functions of wetlands, including their role as carbon sinks and habitats for wildlife. Furthermore, intensive aquaculture practices can lead to water pollution, as uneaten feed and waste accumulate in ponds and are discharged into surrounding waters. This contributes to nutrient loading, algal blooms, and the degradation of adjacent ecosystems, such as seagrass meadows and coral reefs.

Sustainable aquaculture practices can help mitigate these impacts. Initiatives such as integrated multi-trophic aquaculture, which combines species with complementary ecological roles, reduce waste and improve efficiency. Additionally, restoring mangroves as part of aquaculture operations can enhance ecosystem services while maintaining productivity. Certification schemes and better regulation also encourage environmentally responsible aquaculture practices.

Tourism and Recreation in Coastal Wetlands

Coastal wetlands are increasingly valued for their aesthetic, recreational, and cultural significance, making them popular destinations for tourism. Activities such as birdwatching, kayaking, and ecotourism in mangroves and tidal marshes provide opportunities for education, recreation, and economic growth. Tourism generates revenue for local communities, supports conservation initiatives, and raises awareness of the importance of protecting these ecosystems.

However, unmanaged or unsustainable tourism can harm coastal wetlands. Overcrowding, the construction of tourism infrastructure, and pollution from visitors can degrade habitats and disrupt wildlife. For example, mangrove forests often suffer from trampling, cutting, and waste disposal associated with tourism activities. Noise and light pollution may disturb migratory birds and other species that rely on these habitats for feeding and nesting.

Ecotourism, when managed sustainably, offers a way to balance economic benefits with conservation. Programs that limit the number of visitors, enforce strict waste management practices, and involve local communities in decision-making can help reduce the environmental footprint of tourism. Educating tourists about the ecological value of wetlands and their vulnerability further promotes sustainable behavior and support for conservation efforts.

Balancing Human Needs and Wetland Sustainability

The interaction between humans and coastal wetlands is a complex balance of benefits and risks. Agriculture, aquaculture, and tourism contribute to livelihoods and economic development, but they can also degrade the ecosystems that sustain them. Striking a balance requires integrating sustainable practices, promoting community involvement, and enforcing regulatory frameworks that prioritize wetland health.

Governments, non-governmental organizations, and local stakeholders all play critical roles in ensuring that human activities in coastal wetlands are managed responsibly. Policies that incentivize sustainable land use, protect critical habitats, and regulate pollution are essential for minimizing the environmental impact of human interactions. Additionally, restoration initiatives that recover degraded wetlands can rebuild resilience and restore lost ecosystem services.

Sustainability Challenges (Habitat Destruction, Pollution)

Coastal wetlands, including mangroves, salt marshes, and tidal flats, face significant sustainability challenges stemming from human activities. Habitat destruction and pollution are two of the most pressing threats to these ecosystems, compromising their ability to provide critical services such as carbon sequestration, biodiversity support, and flood protection. Addressing these challenges is essential for ensuring the long-term health and resilience of coastal wetlands.

Habitat Destruction

Habitat destruction is one of the primary drivers of wetland degradation worldwide. Coastal wetlands are often cleared or altered to make way for agriculture, aquaculture, urban development, and infrastructure projects. These activities disrupt the ecological balance of wetlands, reducing their capacity to support biodiversity and provide essential ecosystem services.

1. Urbanization and Land Reclamation

Urban expansion and land reclamation are major contributors to habitat loss in coastal wetlands. Mangroves and salt marshes are frequently cleared to create space for residential, commercial, and industrial development. These activities not only destroy critical habitats but also disrupt natural processes such as tidal flows and sediment deposition, further weakening wetland ecosystems. For example, land reclamation often involves draining wetlands, which releases stored carbon into the atmosphere, contributing to greenhouse gas emissions.

2. Aquaculture and Agriculture

The conversion of wetlands into aquaculture ponds and agricultural land is another significant cause of habitat destruction. Intensive shrimp farming and rice cultivation, for instance, often involve clearing mangroves and altering hydrological systems. This results in the loss of critical habitats for wildlife, reduces carbon sequestration capacity, and increases the vulnerability of coastal areas to flooding and erosion.

3. Infrastructure Development

Hard infrastructure, such as seawalls, roads, and ports, further encroaches on wetland areas. These structures fragment habitats, block tidal flows, and limit the ability of wetlands to adapt to rising sea levels. As a result, the resilience of these ecosystems is significantly reduced, making them less effective in providing natural defenses against climate impacts.

Pollution

Pollution poses another major sustainability challenge for coastal wetlands. Pollutants from agricultural runoff, industrial discharges, and urban wastewater degrade water quality and harm wetland ecosystems. The accumulation of pollutants can disrupt ecological processes, reduce biodiversity, and compromise the ability of wetlands to deliver essential services.

1. Nutrient Pollution and Eutrophication

Excessive nutrient inputs from fertilizers and animal waste lead to nutrient pollution in coastal waters. This often results in eutrophication, where increased nutrient levels cause algal blooms that deplete oxygen in the water. These hypoxic conditions can kill fish, shellfish, and other aquatic organisms, disrupting food webs and reducing biodiversity. Eutrophication also affects the health of wetland vegetation, which is critical for stabilizing sediments and maintaining water quality.

2. Industrial and Chemical Pollution

Industrial activities introduce heavy metals, toxins, and chemicals into coastal wetlands. These pollutants accumulate in sediments and organisms, impacting the health of both ecosystems and human communities that rely on these areas for food and water. Persistent organic pollutants can bioaccumulate in wetland species, posing risks to higher trophic levels, including humans.

3. Plastic Pollution

Plastics, including microplastics, are increasingly recognized as a threat to wetland ecosystems. Plastic debris can entangle wildlife, damage vegetation, and alter sediment composition. Microplastics, which are ingested by aquatic organisms, have the potential to disrupt reproductive and physiological processes, further reducing biodiversity and ecosystem health.

Compounding Effects

The combination of habitat destruction and pollution creates compounding effects that further threaten the sustainability of coastal wetlands. For example, polluted wetlands are less resilient to the impacts of habitat loss, as degraded water quality weakens vegetation and reduces the ability of ecosystems to recover. Similarly, fragmented habitats are more vulnerable to the effects of pollution, as they lack the connectivity needed to support diverse species and ecological processes.

Management Strategies for Sustainable Wetland Use

Sustainable management of coastal wetlands is essential for balancing human needs with ecological conservation. Wetlands provide critical services such as carbon sequestration, biodiversity support, and flood protection, but they are increasingly under threat from habitat destruction, pollution, and unsustainable resource use. Effective management strategies can help preserve these ecosystems, ensuring their long-term functionality and resilience while supporting the livelihoods of communities that depend on them.

Ecosystem-Based Management

Ecosystem-based management (EBM) is a holistic approach that focuses on maintaining the health and functionality of entire ecosystems rather than managing individual resources or species. For coastal wetlands, EBM integrates ecological, social, and economic considerations to ensure sustainable use.

• **Restoration of Degraded Ecosystems**: Restoring mangroves, salt marshes, and seagrass meadows enhances their ability to provide ecosystem services such as carbon storage and flood protection. Techniques include replanting vegetation, reconnecting wetlands to tidal flows, and removing invasive species that disrupt native habitats.

• **Protecting Critical Habitats**: Establishing protected areas for wetlands helps safeguard key ecosystems from development and overexploitation. MPAs and buffer zones can limit harmful activities while allowing natural processes to continue.

Sustainable Resource Use

Many communities depend on coastal wetlands for resources such as fish, timber, and agricultural land. Sustainable resource management ensures that these activities do not degrade wetland ecosystems.

• **Sustainable Fishing and Aquaculture**: Implementing regulated fishing practices and promoting sustainable aquaculture reduces overexploitation and minimizes environmental impacts. For example, integrated multi-trophic aquaculture combines species with complementary roles to create a balanced and efficient system.

• **Selective Logging and Agroforestry**: Instead of large-scale clearing, sustainable timber extraction and agroforestry practices allow for the use of mangrove wood and other resources without destroying entire habitats. These approaches preserve biodiversity while providing economic benefits.

Pollution Control and Water Quality Management

Maintaining water quality is critical for the health of coastal wetlands. Pollution from agricultural runoff, industrial discharges, and urban waste threatens these ecosystems, reducing their ability to function effectively.

• **Reducing Nutrient Runoff**: Adopting precision agriculture techniques and reducing fertilizer use minimizes nutrient pollution. Buffer strips of vegetation along waterways can also filter runoff before it reaches wetlands.

• **Improving Wastewater Treatment**: Enhanced treatment of urban and industrial wastewater reduces the input of harmful pollutants, such as heavy metals and organic waste, into wetland systems. Policies that enforce stricter wastewater regulations can significantly improve water quality.

Climate Adaptation Strategies

Coastal wetlands are particularly vulnerable to the impacts of climate change, such as rising sea levels, warming temperatures, and increased storm intensity. Adaptive management strategies can help wetlands cope with these challenges.

• **Facilitating Wetland Migration**: Rising sea levels may submerge wetlands, but providing space for wetlands to migrate inland ensures their survival. This can be achieved through land-use planning that prioritizes conservation and avoids building hard infrastructure near wetlands.

• **Restoring Hydrological Balance**: Maintaining or restoring natural water flows allows wetlands to adapt to changing conditions. For example, reconnecting tidal wetlands to their waterways ensures the flow of nutrients and sediments necessary for wetland health.

Community Engagement and Education

Local communities play a critical role in the sustainable use of wetlands. Engaging communities in conservation efforts ensures that strategies are locally relevant and effective.

• **Participatory Planning**: Involving stakeholders in decision-making processes helps balance conservation goals with the needs of local communities. For example, co-management programs that involve local fishers and farmers in wetland restoration foster a sense of ownership and responsibility.

• **Environmental Education**: Raising awareness about the ecological importance of wetlands encourages sustainable behavior. Educational campaigns, community workshops, and ecotourism initiatives can help people understand the value of wetlands and the consequences of their degradation.

Policy and Governance

Effective policies and governance frameworks are essential for managing wetlands sustainably. Governments and organizations must implement regulations and incentives that encourage conservation and sustainable use.

• **Incentives for Conservation**: Programs such as PES reward landowners and communities for maintaining healthy wetlands. Carbon credits for restored blue carbon ecosystems provide financial incentives for conservation.

• **International and National Frameworks**: Integrating wetlands into climate strategies, such as NDCs under the Paris Agreement, and enforcing national wetland protection laws ensure coordinated efforts to preserve these ecosystems.

Chapter 5: Nature-Based Solutions for Coastal Resilience

NBS are increasingly recognized as essential strategies for enhancing coastal resilience in the face of climate change and human-induced pressures. These approaches leverage natural processes and ecosystems to address challenges such as flooding, erosion, and biodiversity loss while providing co-benefits for communities and the environment. Unlike traditional engineered solutions, which often require high costs and extensive maintenance, NBS offer adaptive, sustainable, and multifunctional alternatives.

This chapter explores the role of nature-based solutions in building resilient coastal systems. It examines key NBS strategies, such as restoring mangroves, creating living shorelines, and rehabilitating seagrass meadows, highlighting their ability to protect coastlines, store carbon, and support biodiversity. The chapter also discusses the integration of NBS with policy, planning, and community engagement to maximize their effectiveness. By embracing NBS, we can enhance the resilience of coastal areas, ensure sustainable development, and address the interconnected challenges posed by climate change and ecosystem degradation.

Introduction to Nature-Based Solutions in Coastal Systems

NBS are innovative approaches that utilize natural ecosystems and processes to address environmental challenges while providing co-benefits for people and biodiversity. In the context of coastal systems, NBS are designed to mitigate the impacts of climate change, such as rising sea levels, storm surges, and erosion, while enhancing ecosystem health and supporting local communities. These solutions offer an adaptive, sustainable alternative to traditional "grey" infrastructure, such as seawalls and levees, which can often disrupt natural processes and require significant maintenance.

Coastal ecosystems, such as mangroves, salt marshes, and seagrass meadows, form the foundation of NBS in coastal systems. These habitats play a vital role in buffering coastlines from extreme weather events, stabilizing sediments, and providing critical ecosystem services, such as carbon sequestration and biodiversity support. Unlike engineered structures, natural ecosystems are dynamic and self-repairing, capable of adapting to changing environmental conditions over time.

One of the core principles of NBS is their multifunctionality. While they address immediate challenges like coastal protection, they also deliver additional benefits, such as improving water quality, supporting fisheries, and offering recreational and cultural opportunities. For example, restoring mangrove forests not only reduces wave energy and prevents erosion but also provides habitat for fish and crabs that sustain local economies.

Incorporating NBS into coastal resilience strategies aligns with global frameworks such as the United Nations SDGs and the Paris Agreement, which emphasize the need for sustainable, nature-based approaches to climate adaptation and mitigation. These solutions are particularly valuable in vulnerable coastal areas, where communities are often highly dependent on natural resources and exposed to the risks of climate change.

Despite their potential, the implementation of NBS faces challenges. Habitat degradation, land-use conflicts, and limited financial and technical resources can hinder efforts to restore or conserve natural ecosystems. Additionally, integrating NBS into existing planning and policy frameworks requires collaboration across multiple sectors, including government agencies, non-governmental organizations, scientists, and local communities.

Examples of Nature-Based Solutions (Restored Mangroves, Oyster Reefs, Living Shorelines)

NBS offer sustainable and multifunctional strategies for addressing climate change impacts in coastal areas. Among the most effective examples are restored mangroves, oyster reefs, and living shorelines. These solutions harness the power of natural ecosystems to provide coastal protection, enhance biodiversity, and support community resilience, while also addressing global climate goals such as carbon sequestration and habitat restoration.

Restored Mangroves

Mangroves are salt-tolerant trees and shrubs that grow in tropical and subtropical coastal zones. They are renowned for their ability to protect shorelines from erosion, reduce wave energy, and act as natural buffers against storm surges and flooding. Mangrove restoration involves replanting degraded or cleared mangrove forests, often in areas where they have been lost due to urban development, aquaculture, or agriculture.

• **Coastal Protection**: The dense root systems of mangroves stabilize sediments, reducing erosion and maintaining shoreline integrity. During storms, mangroves act as a natural barrier, absorbing wave energy and reducing the impact on inland areas.

• **Carbon Sequestration**: Mangroves are highly efficient blue carbon ecosystems, storing large amounts of carbon in their biomass and waterlogged soils. Restoration efforts contribute to climate mitigation by enhancing this carbon sequestration capacity.

• **Biodiversity Support**: Mangroves provide critical habitat for a wide range of species, including fish, crustaceans, and migratory birds. Restoring these ecosystems benefits local fisheries and supports global biodiversity conservation.

• **Community Benefits**: In many regions, mangrove restoration also supports livelihoods by improving fisheries and creating opportunities for ecotourism. For example, community-led mangrove planting projects have been successful in countries such as

Indonesia, where local populations are directly involved in reforestation and benefit from the restored ecosystem services.

Oyster Reefs

Oyster reefs are another powerful example of NBS, offering significant benefits for coastal protection, water quality improvement, and biodiversity. These reefs are formed by the accumulation of oyster shells, which create complex, three-dimensional structures that support marine life and provide natural defenses against coastal hazards.

• **Wave Energy Reduction**: Oyster reefs act as breakwaters, dissipating wave energy and reducing the impact of storm surges on coastal areas. This helps prevent erosion and protects critical infrastructure and habitats.

• **Water Quality Improvement**: Oysters are filter feeders, capable of filtering large volumes of water daily. A single oyster can filter up to 50 gallons of water per day, removing excess nutrients, sediment, and pollutants from the water column. Restoring oyster reefs improves water clarity and supports healthier marine ecosystems.

• **Habitat Creation**: Oyster reefs provide habitat for a variety of marine species, including fish, crabs, and other invertebrates. This enhances biodiversity and supports fisheries that depend on these habitats.

• **Restoration Initiatives**: Oyster reef restoration projects have been implemented in many coastal regions, including the United States, where organizations like The Nature Conservancy have established reef-building programs. These initiatives often involve recycling oyster shells from restaurants and hatcheries to create new reef structures.

Living Shorelines

Living shorelines are hybrid NBS that combine natural elements, such as vegetation and shellfish beds, with minimal engineering to protect coastal areas. Unlike traditional hard infrastructure, such as seawalls, living shorelines are dynamic and adaptable, allowing for the natural movement of water and sediments while providing coastal protection.

• **Erosion Control**: Living shorelines stabilize sediments and reduce erosion by using natural materials like marsh grasses, coir logs, and submerged aquatic vegetation. These elements trap sediments and dissipate wave energy, protecting shorelines from the effects of tides and storms.

• **Habitat Enhancement**: By incorporating native plants, shellfish beds, and submerged structures, living shorelines provide critical habitat for fish, crabs, birds, and other wildlife. This supports local biodiversity and improves ecosystem health.

• **Resilience to Climate Change**: Living shorelines are designed to adapt to changing environmental conditions, such as rising sea levels and increased storm intensity. Unlike static seawalls, they grow and evolve over time, enhancing their long-term effectiveness.

• **Community and Economic Benefits**: Living shorelines can also provide recreational and aesthetic value, attracting tourists and supporting local economies. Additionally, they are often less expensive to install and maintain than traditional infrastructure.

Interconnected Benefits

These three examples of NBS—restored mangroves, oyster reefs, and living shorelines—demonstrate the interconnected benefits of nature-based approaches. By addressing multiple challenges simultaneously, such as coastal protection, water quality, and habitat restoration, these solutions contribute to both local resilience and global sustainability goals. Moreover, they foster community engagement, as many restoration projects actively involve local populations in planning, implementation, and monitoring.

Challenges and Considerations

While these NBS examples are highly effective, their implementation requires careful planning and consideration of local contexts. Factors such as site selection, environmental conditions, and long-term maintenance must be addressed to ensure success. Additionally, funding and policy support are essential for scaling up these solutions to meet growing climate and resilience challenges.

Co-Benefits of Nature-Based Solutions (Biodiversity, Disaster Risk Reduction)

NBS offer a wide range of co-benefits that extend beyond their primary objectives of addressing climate and environmental challenges. Among the most significant are their contributions to biodiversity and disaster risk reduction. These interrelated benefits highlight the value of NBS as multifunctional strategies that enhance both ecological health and human well-being while supporting long-term resilience in coastal areas.

Biodiversity Enhancement

Nature-based solutions, such as restored mangroves, seagrass meadows, and oyster reefs, play a crucial role in preserving and enhancing biodiversity. Coastal ecosystems are some of the most biodiverse habitats on Earth, providing critical support for marine, terrestrial, and migratory species.

1. **Habitat Creation and Restoration**

NBS projects often focus on restoring degraded ecosystems, which creates and improves habitats for a wide variety of species. For instance:

- **Mangroves** provide shelter and breeding grounds for fish, crustaceans, and mollusks, many of which are commercially and ecologically valuable.

- **Seagrass meadows** serve as nurseries for juvenile fish, offering food and protection from predators.

- **Oyster reefs** create complex structures that host diverse communities of invertebrates, fish, and algae, supporting entire food webs.

By restoring these habitats, NBS contribute to the recovery of species populations and the overall health of coastal ecosystems.

2. Support for Migratory Species

Many coastal ecosystems supported by NBS are vital for migratory birds and marine species. Salt marshes, mudflats, and mangroves serve as stopover points for migratory birds, providing food and resting areas during long journeys. Similarly, seagrass meadows and coral reefs are essential for species that migrate across oceans, such as sea turtles and certain fish.

3. Increased Ecosystem Connectivity

NBS often enhance the connectivity between ecosystems, such as linking wetlands with adjacent coral reefs or seagrass meadows. This connectivity allows species to move freely between habitats, supporting ecological processes like feeding, breeding, and migration. Improved connectivity strengthens ecosystems' overall resilience to disturbances, such as storms or habitat loss.

4. Conservation of Endangered Species

By protecting and restoring critical habitats, NBS also help safeguard endangered species. For example, mangrove restoration supports species like the Bengal tiger in the Sundarbans, while seagrass restoration benefits the dugong and green sea turtle. These efforts contribute to global biodiversity conservation targets and reinforce the importance of ecosystems in supporting rare and vulnerable species.

Disaster Risk Reduction

Another key co-benefit of NBS is their role in reducing disaster risks. Coastal communities are increasingly vulnerable to extreme weather events, rising sea levels, and other climate-related hazards. NBS provide natural defenses that protect people, infrastructure, and ecosystems from these threats.

1. Storm Surge Mitigation

Coastal ecosystems such as mangroves and salt marshes act as natural buffers against storm surges. Their dense vegetation absorbs wave energy, reducing the height and intensity of waves before they reach inland areas. For example, mangrove forests can reduce wave heights by as much as 60%, providing critical protection during hurricanes and typhoons.

2. Flood Control

Wetlands and tidal marshes play a significant role in flood mitigation by absorbing and storing excess water during heavy rainfall or storm events. This natural flood control reduces the pressure on built infrastructure, such as levees and drainage systems, and minimizes economic losses from flood damage.

3. Erosion Prevention

NBS help stabilize coastlines and prevent erosion, which is a growing concern due to rising sea levels and increased wave activity. The root systems of mangroves and marsh grasses anchor sediments, reducing their susceptibility to being washed away. Similarly, oyster reefs act as breakwaters, dissipating wave energy and protecting shorelines from erosion.

4. Adaptation to Sea-Level Rise

Unlike hard infrastructure, NBS are adaptive and can respond to gradual changes in environmental conditions, such as sea-level rise. For example, salt marshes and mangroves can migrate inland or accumulate sediment to keep pace with rising water levels. This adaptive capacity ensures that these ecosystems continue to provide protective services over time.

5. Reduction in Heat and Urban Flooding

In coastal urban areas, NBS such as restored wetlands and urban mangroves help moderate temperatures and manage stormwater runoff. This reduces the risks of heat stress and urban flooding, making cities more resilient to climate change.

Interconnected Benefits

The co-benefits of biodiversity enhancement and disaster risk reduction are closely linked. Biodiverse ecosystems are more resilient to disturbances, meaning they are better able to recover from extreme weather events and continue providing protective services. At the same time, by reducing disaster risks, NBS create safer environments for both humans and wildlife, fostering coexistence and long-term sustainability.

Challenges in Scaling Up and Integrating Nature-Based Solutions

NBS hold immense potential for addressing climate change, enhancing biodiversity, and supporting coastal resilience. However, scaling up and integrating NBS into mainstream coastal management and policy frameworks presents several challenges. These obstacles range from financial and technical constraints to governance and societal acceptance. Addressing these challenges is critical to unlocking the full potential of NBS and ensuring their widespread adoption.

Financial Constraints

One of the most significant challenges in scaling up NBS is the lack of adequate funding. While NBS are often more cost-effective than traditional engineered solutions in the long term, they require upfront investment in restoration, monitoring, and maintenance. Governments and private sector stakeholders may prioritize short-term, infrastructure-driven solutions over NBS due to limited budgets or immediate pressure to address coastal hazards. Additionally, funding mechanisms for NBS are not yet well-developed in many regions, and economic incentives such as carbon credits or ecosystem service payments are often underutilized.

Knowledge and Technical Barriers

Implementing NBS requires specialized knowledge of ecological processes, coastal dynamics, and restoration techniques. Limited technical expertise in designing, implementing, and monitoring NBS can hinder their adoption. For instance, restoring mangroves or constructing living shorelines requires site-specific knowledge to ensure success, such as understanding hydrological patterns, sediment dynamics, and plant species suitability. Furthermore, long-term monitoring is essential to assess the effectiveness of NBS, but many projects lack the technical capacity or resources to conduct this monitoring effectively.

Land Use Conflicts

Competition for land and coastal space poses a significant barrier to scaling up NBS. Coastal areas are often highly developed or used for agriculture, aquaculture, and tourism. Integrating NBS into these spaces may require trade-offs that are not always acceptable to local stakeholders. For example, restoring wetlands might involve converting agricultural land back into natural habitats, which can be met with resistance from farmers. Addressing these conflicts requires careful planning, stakeholder engagement, and policies that prioritize conservation and sustainable land use.

Policy and Governance Challenges

The integration of NBS into national and local policies is often limited by fragmented governance structures and a lack of coordination among stakeholders. Coastal management typically involves multiple sectors, including urban planning, environmental protection, and disaster management, which can lead to conflicting priorities. Policies that support NBS, such as incentives for restoration or regulations to protect critical habitats, are often underdeveloped or poorly enforced. Additionally, NBS are sometimes viewed as supplementary rather than primary solutions, leading to underinvestment in their implementation.

Social and Cultural Acceptance

Public awareness and acceptance of NBS can also be a barrier. Many communities and decision-makers are more familiar with traditional engineered solutions, such as seawalls, and may perceive NBS as less reliable. Changing perceptions requires education, demonstration projects, and communication efforts to showcase the effectiveness and co-benefits of NBS. Additionally, engaging local communities in the design and implementation of NBS is essential to building trust and ensuring that these solutions meet societal needs.

Uncertainty and Climate Change

The uncertainty associated with climate change adds complexity to scaling up NBS. Rising sea levels, changing weather patterns, and other climate-related impacts can affect the long-term viability of NBS, making it difficult to predict their performance in certain conditions. Adaptive management approaches, which involve continuous monitoring and adjustments, are essential but require additional resources and capacity.

Chapter 6: Technological Advances in Coastal Resilience

Technological advancements are transforming the way we understand, manage, and enhance coastal resilience. From satellite monitoring to predictive modeling and innovative engineering solutions, technology provides critical tools for addressing the complex challenges faced by coastal regions. These tools complement nature-based solutions and traditional management practices, enabling data-driven decision-making, real-time monitoring, and more effective adaptation strategies.

This chapter explores the role of technology in building resilient coastal systems, focusing on its applications in monitoring, forecasting, and adaptive management. It examines cutting-edge innovations such as remote sensing, artificial intelligence (AI), and autonomous monitoring systems, alongside emerging techniques in green engineering and coastal infrastructure design. By integrating these technologies with ecological and community-based approaches, we can better prepare for and respond to the growing threats posed by climate change, human activities, and natural disasters. Ultimately, technological advances are key to achieving sustainable, adaptive, and resilient coastal systems.

Role of Technology in Coastal Monitoring (AI, GIS, Remote Sensing)

Technological advancements in coastal monitoring have significantly enhanced our ability to understand, predict, and manage changes in coastal environments. Tools such as AI, geographic information systems (GIS), and remote sensing provide critical insights into coastal dynamics, enabling data-driven decision-making and adaptive management. These technologies complement traditional monitoring methods, offering greater efficiency, precision, and scalability to address the growing challenges of coastal resilience.

AI in Coastal Monitoring

AI has revolutionized the way we collect, analyze, and interpret coastal data. Machine learning algorithms, a subset of AI, can process vast amounts of data from multiple sources, identifying patterns and trends that may not be immediately apparent through conventional methods.

1. Predictive Modeling

AI-powered models are increasingly used to predict coastal hazards such as storm surges, sea-level rise, and shoreline erosion. By analyzing historical data and real-time inputs, these models can forecast potential risks with high accuracy. For instance, AI can simulate the impacts of extreme weather events on coastal systems, helping communities prepare for and mitigate damage.

2. Automated Data Analysis

AI algorithms are employed to process data from satellites, drones, and sensors, automating tasks such as mapping shoreline changes, detecting habitat loss, and monitoring water quality. This reduces the time and resources needed for manual analysis while improving accuracy and consistency.

3. Real-Time Monitoring

AI enhances real-time monitoring systems by integrating data from various sources, such as weather stations and ocean buoys. For example, AI-powered systems can detect anomalies, such as unusual wave patterns or temperature changes, and issue early warnings to mitigate risks.

4. Ecosystem Monitoring

AI is used to assess the health of coastal ecosystems, including mangroves, coral reefs, and seagrass meadows. Image recognition algorithms analyze aerial and underwater imagery to identify signs of degradation, such as bleaching in corals or deforestation in mangroves.

GIS

GIS is a powerful tool for visualizing, analyzing, and managing spatial data, making it indispensable for coastal monitoring and planning. It integrates information from various sources, such as satellite imagery, field surveys, and historical records, to create comprehensive maps and models.

1. Mapping and Visualization

GIS enables detailed mapping of coastal features, including shorelines, wetlands, and bathymetry. These maps provide a clear visual representation of changes over time, such as erosion, land use changes, or habitat loss. Interactive GIS platforms allow decision-makers to overlay multiple data layers, such as population density, flood zones, and infrastructure, to assess risks and plan interventions.

2. Monitoring Coastal Changes

GIS is widely used to monitor shoreline changes and sediment dynamics. By comparing historical and current data, it can identify areas at risk of erosion or accretion, informing strategies for coastal protection.

3. Scenario Analysis

GIS supports scenario-based planning by modeling the impacts of different management actions or climate scenarios. For instance, GIS tools can simulate the effects of sea-level rise on wetlands or predict the outcomes of mangrove restoration projects.

4. Disaster Risk Assessment

GIS is instrumental in assessing disaster risks and planning evacuation routes. By integrating hazard data with population and infrastructure maps, GIS can identify vulnerable areas and prioritize mitigation efforts.

Remote Sensing in Coastal Monitoring

Remote sensing involves the collection of data from satellites, drones, and other aerial platforms, providing a bird's-eye view of coastal environments. This technology enables large-scale monitoring of coastal systems with high spatial and temporal resolution.

1. Satellite Imaging

Satellites equipped with optical and radar sensors capture detailed images of coastal regions, enabling continuous monitoring of changes in land cover, vegetation, and water bodies. For example, satellite imagery is used to track the expansion of urban areas, the loss of wetlands, or the growth of harmful algal blooms.

2. Drones and Aerial Surveys

Drones are increasingly used for high-resolution monitoring of coastal ecosystems. They can capture imagery at finer scales than satellites, making them ideal for assessing small-scale changes, such as erosion along shorelines or damage to mangrove forests. Drones are also cost-effective and flexible, allowing for targeted surveys in areas that are difficult to access.

3. Water Quality Monitoring

Remote sensing technologies can detect changes in water quality parameters, such as turbidity, chlorophyll levels, and temperature.

For instance, thermal sensors on satellites and drones are used to monitor ocean surface temperatures, which are critical for understanding the impacts of climate change on coastal systems.

4. Sea-Level and Tidal Monitoring

Satellite altimetry measures sea-level changes with high precision, providing critical data for tracking the impacts of climate change. This information is essential for identifying areas at risk of inundation and planning adaptive measures.

Integrating Technologies for Coastal Monitoring

The integration of AI, GIS, and remote sensing creates a comprehensive framework for coastal monitoring. These technologies complement each other, combining the predictive power of AI, the spatial analysis capabilities of GIS, and the large-scale data collection of remote sensing. For example, GIS platforms can incorporate remote sensing data, while AI algorithms analyze these datasets to generate actionable insights.

Challenges and Opportunities

While these technologies offer immense potential, their implementation is not without challenges. High costs, limited technical expertise, and data availability are common barriers, particularly in low-resource settings. However, advancements in technology, such as open-source tools and cloud-based platforms, are reducing these barriers and making coastal monitoring more accessible.

Engineering Innovations (Floating Cities, Storm Surge Barriers)

Engineering innovations are revolutionizing the way coastal communities address challenges posed by climate change and rising sea levels. Floating cities and storm surge barriers represent two cutting-edge solutions that showcase human ingenuity in creating adaptive infrastructure to enhance coastal resilience. These innovations aim to protect vulnerable populations, mitigate disaster risks, and ensure sustainable living in the face of increasingly severe environmental threats.

Floating Cities

Floating cities are an innovative response to the threat of rising sea levels, offering a sustainable and adaptive solution for coastal communities. These engineered habitats are designed to float on water while providing the necessary infrastructure for housing, commerce, and community living. By creating space on the water, floating cities reduce pressure on terrestrial land and provide a unique way to coexist with rising seas.

1. Design and Structure

Floating cities are built on buoyant platforms made of durable and sustainable materials, such as reinforced concrete or modular plastic systems. These platforms are anchored to the seabed or designed to drift with ocean currents, depending on the specific environmental and geographic context. They include essential infrastructure such as housing, transportation networks, renewable energy systems, and waste management facilities.

2. Sustainability Features

Many floating city designs incorporate sustainable technologies to minimize their environmental impact. Renewable energy sources, such as solar panels and wind turbines, power these cities, while advanced wastewater treatment systems recycle water and reduce pollution. Floating farms or vertical agriculture are often integrated to produce food locally, reducing reliance on land-based resources.

3. Adaptation and Resilience

Floating cities are particularly suited to regions prone to sea-level rise and flooding. Their design allows them to rise and fall with changing water levels, ensuring continued functionality during extreme weather events. For example, floating cities could provide safe and sustainable living environments for populations in low-lying island nations or delta regions where land is becoming increasingly uninhabitable.

4. Challenges and Opportunities

While floating cities offer exciting possibilities, their development faces challenges, including high construction costs, regulatory hurdles, and technical complexities. Collaboration among governments, private sectors, and international organizations is critical to scaling up this innovation. Pilot projects, such as Oceanix City supported by the United Nations, demonstrate the feasibility of floating cities and provide valuable insights for future development.

Storm Surge Barriers

Storm surge barriers are large-scale engineering structures designed to protect coastal areas from flooding caused by storm surges and rising seas. These barriers play a critical role in reducing the impacts of extreme weather events, safeguarding lives, infrastructure, and ecosystems.

1. Design and Functionality

Storm surge barriers are typically massive gates or walls built across estuaries, rivers, or coastal zones. They are designed to remain open under normal conditions, allowing water to flow freely and maintaining tidal dynamics. During extreme weather events, such as hurricanes or typhoons, the barriers close to prevent storm surges from inundating coastal areas. Some barriers, like the

Maeslantkering in the Netherlands, operate as movable structures, closing only when necessary.

2. Examples of Implementation

• **The Thames Barrier** in London is one of the most well-known storm surge barriers. It protects the city from tidal flooding by controlling water levels during high tides and storm surges.

• **The Delta Works** in the Netherlands is a series of storm surge barriers and dams designed to protect the low-lying country from flooding. This system combines advanced engineering with environmental considerations to ensure the safety and sustainability of coastal regions.

3. Coastal Protection and Resilience

Storm surge barriers significantly reduce the risk of flooding in densely populated coastal areas, protecting homes, businesses, and critical infrastructure. By mitigating the impacts of extreme weather events, these structures also provide long-term economic benefits by reducing disaster recovery costs and supporting stable development in vulnerable regions.

4. Environmental and Economic Considerations

While effective, storm surge barriers can pose challenges to natural ecosystems by altering tidal flows and sediment transport. To minimize these impacts, modern designs increasingly incorporate features that allow for ecological balance, such as fish passages and sediment bypass systems. The high construction and maintenance costs of storm surge barriers also require careful planning and investment.

Hybrid Approaches Combining Technology and Nature-Based Solutions

Hybrid approaches that integrate technology with NBS offer innovative strategies for enhancing coastal resilience. By combining the adaptive and self-sustaining benefits of natural systems with the precision and efficiency of technological tools, these approaches maximize the effectiveness of coastal protection, restoration, and management. Hybrid solutions address complex challenges such as rising sea levels, erosion, and storm surges, while simultaneously supporting biodiversity, improving water quality, and fostering community resilience.

Living Shorelines with Integrated Monitoring Systems

Living shorelines are a nature-based alternative to traditional seawalls, incorporating vegetation, shellfish reefs, and other natural elements to stabilize coastlines and reduce erosion. By integrating technology, such as real-time monitoring systems, these solutions become more adaptive and effective.

• **Real-Time Data Collection**: Sensors and drones can monitor environmental conditions, such as wave energy, sediment movement, and vegetation health. This data allows for ongoing assessment and adjustments to the design and maintenance of living shorelines.

• **Wave Energy Dissipation**: Combining natural elements like oyster reefs with engineered structures, such as anchored coir logs or geotextile barriers, enhances the ability to dissipate wave energy during storms. This hybrid approach balances ecological restoration with reliable coastal protection.

• **Case Example**: Projects like the hybrid living shorelines in Chesapeake Bay, USA, demonstrate how natural marsh grasses and oyster reefs, supplemented with minimal engineering, protect shorelines while maintaining ecological functionality.

Restored Wetlands with AI-Driven Management

Restored wetlands are critical for carbon sequestration, flood mitigation, and habitat restoration. Incorporating AI into their management ensures these ecosystems remain effective under changing environmental conditions.

• **Predictive Modeling**: AI algorithms analyze historical data and current environmental factors to predict potential challenges, such as sea-level rise or extreme weather events. This enables proactive adjustments to wetland restoration projects.

• **Water Flow Optimization**: Technology like remote-controlled water gates or automated tidal flow systems helps maintain optimal hydrological conditions in restored wetlands, preventing flooding while supporting ecosystem health.

• **Monitoring Ecosystem Health**: AI-driven image recognition software assesses wetland vegetation growth, soil quality, and water quality, providing detailed insights into ecosystem performance. This data informs adaptive management strategies.

Mangrove Restoration Enhanced by Remote Sensing

Mangroves are highly effective in reducing storm surge impacts, preventing erosion, and storing carbon. Remote sensing technologies, such as satellite imagery and drones, enhance mangrove restoration efforts by enabling precise planning and monitoring.

• **Site Selection and Mapping**: Remote sensing identifies suitable locations for mangrove planting, considering factors like sediment composition, tidal range, and salinity. This ensures restoration efforts are targeted and effective.

• **Growth Monitoring**: High-resolution satellite imagery and drones track mangrove growth over time, allowing stakeholders to assess the success of restoration projects and address challenges such as disease or human interference.

• **Integrated Engineering Solutions**: Hybrid projects may include low-impact structures, such as wave attenuation devices, to stabilize sediment and create favorable conditions for mangrove establishment.

Coral Reef Restoration with Marine Robotics

Coral reefs are vital for protecting coastlines, supporting fisheries, and maintaining biodiversity. Hybrid approaches combine natural coral restoration with technological innovations like marine robotics and 3D printing.

• **Artificial Reef Structures**: 3D-printed reef modules provide stable substrates for coral growth, mimicking the complexity of natural reefs. These structures enhance biodiversity while offering immediate wave protection.

• **Robotic Coral Planting**: Autonomous underwater vehicles (AUVs) are used to plant coral fragments efficiently across large areas, significantly speeding up restoration efforts compared to manual methods.

• **Integrated Monitoring**: Sensors deployed around coral reefs monitor water temperature, acidity, and pollution levels, ensuring that restoration projects are adjusted to changing conditions.

Combining Green and Grey Infrastructure

Hybrid approaches often integrate NBS with traditional engineered solutions, known as "green-grey" infrastructure. This combination provides the durability of engineered structures with the adaptability and co-benefits of natural systems.

• **Wave Attenuation**: For example, a seawall can be fronted by a restored marsh or mangrove forest, which absorbs wave energy and reduces maintenance costs for the engineered structure.

• **Sediment Management**: Hybrid systems can include engineered sediment traps that enhance natural processes like sediment deposition in wetlands or marshes, promoting their growth and long-term stability.

• **Flood Control**: Green-grey solutions like flood retention basins combined with vegetated buffers offer superior flood mitigation compared to traditional infrastructure alone.

Community Engagement and Co-Benefits

Hybrid approaches not only enhance coastal resilience but also provide co-benefits such as improved fisheries, carbon sequestration, and recreational opportunities. Engaging local communities in the planning and implementation of these projects ensures long-term sustainability and social acceptance.

Challenges of Adopting Advanced Technologies

The adoption of advanced technologies for coastal resilience, such AI, remote sensing, and predictive modeling, holds significant promise for improving the management and protection of coastal systems. However, implementing these technologies comes with several challenges that must be addressed to fully realize their potential. These challenges include financial barriers, technical expertise gaps, data limitations, and societal acceptance issues, which collectively influence the effectiveness and scalability of these tools.

Financial Barriers

One of the most prominent challenges is the high cost associated with developing, implementing, and maintaining advanced technologies. The initial investment required for sophisticated tools such as satellite systems, AI-driven software, and autonomous monitoring devices can be prohibitively expensive, particularly for developing countries and small coastal communities. Additionally, ongoing operational and maintenance costs may strain limited budgets, making it difficult to sustain these technologies over the long term. Securing funding from governments, private investors, or international organizations is often a prerequisite for adoption, but such support can be inconsistent or insufficient.

Limited Technical Expertise

The implementation of advanced technologies requires specialized knowledge and skills that may not be readily available in many coastal regions. Operating and maintaining systems such as drones, AI-powered platforms, and GIS mapping tools often necessitate extensive training and expertise. In many cases, local capacity-building efforts are insufficient to bridge the gap, leading to reliance on external experts or organizations. This dependency can hinder the scalability and sustainability of technological solutions, particularly in low-resource settings.

Data Limitations and Accessibility

Effective use of advanced technologies relies on the availability and quality of data, which can be a significant obstacle. For instance:

• **Data Gaps**: Coastal regions, particularly in developing countries, often lack baseline data on shoreline dynamics, ecosystem health, or historical climate trends, making it difficult to calibrate and validate technological models.

• **Fragmented Data Sources**: Data is often scattered across multiple organizations or platforms, leading to inefficiencies in integrating and analyzing information.

• **Data Costs**: Accessing high-resolution satellite imagery, advanced modeling software, or real-time monitoring systems often requires financial resources that may not be available to all stakeholders.

Improving data sharing and accessibility is critical for addressing these limitations.

Governance and Policy Challenges

Integrating advanced technologies into coastal management plans often requires supportive governance structures and policy frameworks, which are not always in place. Regulations governing the use of drones, data privacy laws, and cross-sector collaboration can complicate the implementation process. Furthermore, a lack of standardized practices for deploying these technologies across regions creates inconsistencies in their application and effectiveness.

Societal Acceptance

Public and stakeholder acceptance of advanced technologies can also pose challenges. Communities may perceive these tools as overly complex, intrusive, or disconnected from traditional knowledge and practices. For example, reliance on AI-driven predictions may be met with skepticism if the rationale behind decisions is not clearly communicated. Building trust through transparency, education, and participatory approaches is essential for fostering acceptance and ensuring the successful adoption of these technologies.

Climate Change and Uncertainty

The unpredictable nature of climate change adds complexity to the adoption of advanced technologies. As conditions evolve, technologies and models must be frequently updated to remain relevant, requiring additional resources and adaptability. This dynamic nature can make long-term planning and investment decisions more challenging.

Chapter 7: Governance and Policy Frameworks for Coastal Resilience

Effective governance and policy frameworks are critical to advancing coastal resilience in the face of growing environmental challenges. As climate change intensifies and human activities increasingly impact coastal ecosystems, there is an urgent need for coordinated, inclusive, and adaptive approaches to manage these dynamic regions. Governance frameworks provide the structure for integrating diverse stakeholders, balancing competing interests, and ensuring the sustainable use of coastal resources.

This chapter explores the role of governance and policy in enhancing coastal resilience, focusing on the importance of multi-level collaboration among local, national, and international stakeholders. It examines key elements of successful governance, such as participatory decision-making, policy integration, and adaptive management. Additionally, the chapter highlights the importance of regulatory tools, economic incentives, and community engagement in driving effective coastal management. By addressing governance challenges and promoting robust policy frameworks, we can create resilient coastal systems that support both ecological health and human well-being.

Global and Regional Policy Initiatives (SDGs, Paris Agreement)

Global and regional policy initiatives play a pivotal role in advancing coastal resilience by providing frameworks, targets, and collaborative platforms for addressing the multifaceted challenges facing coastal systems. These initiatives guide efforts to mitigate climate change, conserve biodiversity, and promote sustainable development. Two of the most influential global frameworks are the United Nations SDGs and the Paris Agreement, while various regional initiatives address specific coastal challenges in localized contexts.

United Nations SDGs

The SDGs, adopted by the United Nations in 2015, provide a comprehensive framework for addressing global challenges, including those affecting coastal resilience. Several goals directly or indirectly support the sustainable management of coastal systems.

• Goal 13: Climate Action

SDG 13 calls for urgent action to combat climate change and its impacts. This goal emphasizes the need to strengthen adaptive capacity and resilience in coastal regions, which are particularly vulnerable to rising sea levels, extreme weather events, and other climate-related hazards. Policies and projects under this goal often prioritize NBS, such as mangrove restoration and wetland conservation, to protect coastal areas.

• Goal 14: Life Below Water

SDG 14 focuses on conserving and sustainably using oceans, seas, and marine resources. It includes targets for reducing marine pollution, protecting marine ecosystems, and increasing scientific knowledge to enhance ocean health. Coastal resilience efforts align with this goal through initiatives such as preventing habitat destruction, improving water quality, and ensuring the sustainable management of fisheries and coastal ecosystems.

• Goal 15: Life on Land

SDG 15 addresses the protection and restoration of terrestrial and coastal ecosystems. This goal underscores the importance of sustainable land use, combating desertification, and restoring degraded habitats, including coastal wetlands and mangroves, which play critical roles in coastal resilience.

Paris Agreement

The Paris Agreement, adopted in 2015 under the United Nations Framework Convention on Climate Change (UNFCCC), is a landmark international accord aimed at limiting global warming to well below 2°C, with efforts to restrict it to 1.5°C. The agreement emphasizes the importance of adaptation, resilience, and mitigation efforts, particularly for vulnerable coastal regions.

• NDCs

The Paris Agreement requires countries to submit NDCs outlining their climate goals and strategies. Many nations include coastal resilience measures in their NDCs, such as restoring blue carbon ecosystems (mangroves, salt marshes, and seagrasses) and implementing hybrid solutions that combine technology and NBS. These measures contribute to both climate adaptation and mitigation by enhancing natural carbon sinks and protecting vulnerable coastal populations.

• Global Climate Finance Mechanisms

The Paris Agreement highlights the need for financial support to enable adaptation and resilience efforts in developing countries. Mechanisms such as the Green Climate Fund (GCF) provide funding for coastal resilience projects, including wetland restoration, flood risk management, and sustainable infrastructure development. This financial assistance is critical for scaling up resilience initiatives in low-resource regions.

• Loss and Damage Framework

The Paris Agreement also recognizes the concept of "loss and damage," which addresses the impacts of climate change that cannot be avoided through mitigation or adaptation. Coastal areas, which are particularly vulnerable to sea-level rise and extreme weather events, are often central to loss and damage discussions, with a focus on protecting communities and ecosystems from irreversible harm.

Regional Policy Initiatives

In addition to global frameworks, regional initiatives address specific challenges and priorities for coastal resilience in localized contexts.

• European Union (EU): Integrated Coastal Zone Management (ICZM)

The EU promotes ICZM as a strategic approach to sustainable coastal management, integrating environmental, economic, and social objectives. The EU's Marine Strategy Framework Directive (MSFD) further supports the protection and restoration of marine ecosystems, emphasizing the role of coastal resilience in achieving "good environmental status" for European waters.

• Association of Southeast Asian Nations (ASEAN): Coastal and Marine Environment Programme

ASEAN's program focuses on conserving coastal and marine resources in Southeast Asia, where millions of people depend on these ecosystems for their livelihoods. Initiatives include mangrove restoration, sustainable fisheries management, and capacity-building programs to enhance resilience in member states.

• African Union: African Coastal Resilience Programme

The African Union (AU) addresses coastal resilience through programs that tackle erosion, habitat degradation, and climate impacts. By promoting community-led adaptation projects and nature-based solutions, the AU aims to protect both coastal ecosystems and the livelihoods of vulnerable populations.

• Caribbean Community (CARICOM): Climate Resilience Initiatives

CARICOM countries, highly susceptible to hurricanes and rising sea levels, have adopted regional strategies that prioritize coastal resilience. These include enhancing disaster preparedness, restoring coral reefs and mangroves, and securing international funding for adaptation measures.

Synergies and Challenges

Global and regional policy initiatives often complement each other, creating synergies that amplify the impact of coastal resilience efforts. For example, national policies aligned with the SDGs and Paris Agreement contribute to global climate and sustainability targets while addressing local needs. However, challenges such as inconsistent implementation, limited financial resources, and fragmented governance can hinder the effectiveness of these initiatives. Strengthening collaboration among stakeholders and ensuring policy coherence are essential to overcoming these obstacles.

Challenges in Governance (Coordination, Inclusivity, Equity)

Effective governance is essential for achieving coastal resilience, but it faces numerous challenges that can hinder the implementation of sustainable and adaptive management strategies. Key issues in governance include the lack of coordination among stakeholders, the need for inclusivity in decision-making, and ensuring equitable outcomes for all affected communities. Addressing these challenges is critical for fostering resilient and sustainable coastal systems.

Lack of Coordination

One of the most significant governance challenges is the lack of coordination among the diverse stakeholders involved in coastal management. Coastal resilience efforts typically require input and collaboration from multiple sectors, including government agencies, NGOs, academic institutions, private enterprises, and local communities. However, siloed decision-making and fragmented responsibilities often lead to inefficiencies and missed opportunities for integrated solutions.

• **Overlapping Jurisdictions**: Coastal areas frequently fall under the jurisdiction of multiple levels of government—local, regional, and national—which can result in conflicting policies and priorities. For example, one agency may focus on infrastructure development, while another emphasizes environmental protection, leading to fragmented approaches that fail to address the interconnected nature of coastal systems.

• **Sectoral Silos**: The lack of communication and collaboration between sectors, such as urban planning, environmental conservation, and disaster risk management, further complicates governance. Without a shared vision or coordinated strategy, efforts to enhance coastal resilience may be duplicative or counterproductive.

• **Cross-Border Challenges**: For coastal regions that span multiple countries, such as shared river basins or marine ecosystems, governance coordination becomes even more complex. Differing legal frameworks, resource priorities, and political dynamics can hinder collaborative efforts.

Lack of Inclusivity in Decision-Making

Inclusivity is a cornerstone of effective governance, as it ensures that all stakeholders, particularly marginalized groups, have a voice in decision-making processes. However, many governance frameworks fail to meaningfully involve the diverse range of stakeholders affected by coastal resilience initiatives.

• **Limited Community Engagement**: Local communities, who are often most directly impacted by coastal changes, are frequently excluded from planning and decision-making processes. This can lead to a lack of trust, reduced buy-in, and ineffective implementation of resilience measures. For instance, top-down approaches may overlook local knowledge and cultural practices that are critical for sustainable management.

• **Underrepresentation of Vulnerable Groups**: Women, Indigenous peoples, and economically disadvantaged populations are often underrepresented in governance structures. Their exclusion not only perpetuates inequality but also limits the potential for innovative and context-specific solutions that draw on their unique perspectives and experiences.

• **Power Imbalances**: Coastal governance is often dominated by powerful stakeholders, such as large corporations or government agencies, who may prioritize economic development over environmental conservation or social equity. This can marginalize smaller or less influential voices, resulting in decisions that fail to address the needs of all stakeholders.

Equity Challenges

Equity is a critical consideration in coastal governance, as the impacts of climate change and environmental degradation are not felt equally across populations. Governance frameworks often struggle to address these disparities, resulting in uneven distribution of resources and benefits.

• **Disproportionate Impacts**: Vulnerable populations, such as low-income communities and small-scale fishers, are often disproportionately affected by coastal hazards, such as flooding, erosion, and habitat loss. Governance systems that fail to prioritize these groups exacerbate existing inequalities, leaving them more exposed to risks.

• **Unequal Access to Resources**: Coastal resilience initiatives often require significant financial and technical resources, which may not be equitably distributed. For example, wealthier regions may have access to advanced technologies and infrastructure, while poorer areas are left without adequate support.

• **Benefit Sharing**: Governance frameworks frequently overlook the need to equitably distribute the benefits of coastal resilience projects. For instance, ecotourism initiatives or blue carbon markets may generate economic gains that are not shared with the local communities responsible for conserving these ecosystems.

Overcoming Governance Challenges

Addressing these governance challenges requires targeted efforts to improve coordination, inclusivity, and equity in decision-making processes.

• **Integrated Management**: Establishing ICZM frameworks can help align policies and actions across sectors and jurisdictions. These frameworks promote collaboration and shared responsibility, ensuring that all stakeholders work toward common goals.

• **Participatory Approaches**: Inclusive decision-making processes that actively involve local communities, Indigenous groups, and marginalized populations are essential for building trust and ensuring the effectiveness of resilience measures. Tools such as stakeholder workshops, community consultations, and co-management arrangements can facilitate meaningful participation.

• **Equitable Policies and Funding Mechanisms**: Governance frameworks should prioritize equity by directing resources and support to vulnerable populations. For example, targeted funding mechanisms, such as grants or subsidies for small-scale fishers, can help level the playing field and ensure that resilience initiatives benefit all stakeholders.

Integrating Blue Carbon and Wetland Systems into Policies

Blue carbon ecosystems, such as mangroves, salt marshes, and seagrass meadows, play a critical role in mitigating climate change, enhancing biodiversity, and protecting coastal communities from extreme weather events. Despite their significance, these ecosystems are often underrepresented in policy frameworks. Integrating blue carbon and wetland systems into national and international policies is essential for ensuring their protection, restoration, and sustainable use. Such integration provides opportunities to address climate goals, conserve biodiversity, and support coastal resilience.

Importance of Blue Carbon and Wetland Systems

Blue carbon ecosystems are highly efficient at capturing and storing carbon dioxide from the atmosphere. Mangroves and salt marshes, for example, sequester carbon not only in their biomass but also in their waterlogged soils, where carbon can remain stored for centuries. Beyond carbon storage, these systems provide critical ecosystem services, such as storm surge protection, erosion control, water purification, and habitat for marine and terrestrial species. The benefits they provide underscore the need for their inclusion in policy frameworks to maximize their contribution to environmental, economic, and social well-being.

Current Gaps in Policy

Despite their value, blue carbon ecosystems are often overlooked in national and global policies. Many coastal management frameworks focus on traditional engineering solutions for climate adaptation while neglecting the potential of NBS like wetland restoration. Additionally:

• **Limited Carbon Accounting**: Blue carbon ecosystems are often excluded from national greenhouse gas inventories, which limits their recognition as viable carbon sinks in climate mitigation strategies.

• **Insufficient Protection**: Many countries lack legal protections for blue carbon ecosystems, leaving them vulnerable to destruction from urban development, agriculture, and aquaculture.

• **Fragmented Management**: The management of wetlands and blue carbon ecosystems is often fragmented across sectors, leading to inconsistent policies and conflicting priorities.

Integrating Blue Carbon into Climate Policies

To address these gaps, blue carbon and wetland systems must be systematically integrated into climate policies, such as NDCs under the Paris Agreement. Several key strategies can facilitate this integration:

• **Inclusion in Carbon Accounting**: Incorporating blue carbon ecosystems into carbon accounting frameworks allows countries to quantify their climate mitigation benefits. For example, the restoration of mangroves and salt marshes can be included as nature-based solutions in emissions reduction targets.

• **Support for Restoration Projects**: Policies should prioritize the restoration of degraded blue carbon ecosystems to enhance their carbon sequestration potential. Financial incentives, such as carbon credits, can encourage investments in restoration efforts.

• **Alignment with Global Frameworks**: Linking national policies to global frameworks, such as the United Nations SDGs and the Ramsar Convention on Wetlands, ensures alignment with international conservation and climate goals.

Wetland Systems in Coastal Management Policies

Wetlands play a vital role in coastal resilience and should be incorporated into broader coastal and marine spatial planning policies. Key approaches include:

• **Establishing Legal Protections**: Strengthening legal frameworks to protect wetlands from land conversion and pollution is essential. Protected area designations, such as MPAs or Ramsar sites, can safeguard critical habitats.

• **Incorporating Wetlands into Disaster Risk Reduction**: Policies that integrate wetland restoration into disaster risk reduction strategies can enhance natural defenses against flooding, storm surges, and sea-level rise. For example, wetlands can be designated as buffer zones to absorb excess water during extreme weather events.

• **Promoting Sustainable Use**: Policies should support sustainable wetland use practices, such as community-based fisheries management and ecotourism, that balance conservation with economic benefits.

Challenges and Opportunities

Integrating blue carbon and wetland systems into policies is not without challenges. These include:

• **Data and Monitoring Gaps**: Effective policy integration requires robust data on blue carbon stocks, wetland health, and ecosystem services, which are often lacking in many regions.

• **Coordination Across Sectors**: Managing blue carbon ecosystems requires collaboration among environmental, agricultural, and urban development sectors, which can be difficult to achieve.

• **Funding Constraints**: Limited financial resources can hinder the implementation of wetland protection and restoration policies.

However, opportunities exist to overcome these challenges. Advances in remote sensing and data analytics can improve monitoring and reporting, while international funding mechanisms, such as the GCF, can support blue carbon projects. Engaging local communities and integrating traditional ecological knowledge into policy frameworks can also enhance the success of these initiatives.

Proposing Frameworks for Multi-Stakeholder Collaboration

Coastal resilience requires the collective efforts of diverse stakeholders, including governments, non-governmental organizations (NGOs), private sector entities, academic institutions, and local communities. However, fragmented decision-making and conflicting priorities often hinder effective collaboration. To address these challenges, frameworks for multi-stakeholder collaboration are essential. Such frameworks can facilitate coordinated action, shared responsibilities, and inclusive decision-making, ultimately fostering more sustainable and adaptive coastal management.

Importance of Multi-Stakeholder Collaboration

Coastal systems are dynamic and multifunctional, supporting diverse human and ecological needs. Effective management requires input from multiple sectors and levels of governance. Multi-stakeholder collaboration:

• **Bridges Gaps in Expertise**: Combines the technical knowledge of scientists, the operational capacity of governments, and the on-the-ground experience of local communities.

• **Enhances Resource Efficiency**: Promotes resource-sharing, reduces redundancies, and maximizes the impact of interventions.

• **Increases Buy-In and Ownership**: Ensures that all stakeholders feel invested in and accountable for the outcomes of coastal resilience projects.

Key Components of Collaborative Frameworks

94

Effective multi-stakeholder collaboration frameworks should incorporate the following components:

1. Clear Governance Structures

Defining roles and responsibilities ensures accountability and avoids conflicts. Governance structures can include:

• **Steering Committees**: Comprised of representatives from all stakeholder groups to oversee project implementation and ensure alignment with shared objectives.

• **Advisory Boards**: Including scientists, policy experts, and local leaders to provide technical and contextual guidance.

2. Participatory Decision-Making

Ensuring that all stakeholders have an equal voice fosters inclusivity and fairness. Tools for participatory decision-making include:

• **Stakeholder Consultations**: Regular meetings and workshops to gather input and feedback from diverse groups.

• **Community Forums**: Platforms for local communities to voice concerns, propose solutions, and share traditional knowledge.

3. Shared Goals and Objectives

Establishing common goals promotes alignment among stakeholders. For example, resilience frameworks might include objectives such as protecting critical habitats, reducing coastal vulnerability, and ensuring sustainable livelihoods.

4. Flexible and Adaptive Processes

Given the dynamic nature of coastal systems, frameworks must be flexible to accommodate changing conditions. Adaptive management approaches allow stakeholders to revise strategies based on monitoring and evaluation results.

5. Resource Mobilization

Collaborative frameworks must address funding and resource allocation. Public-private partnerships, international grants, and community contributions can be leveraged to support resilience initiatives.

Examples of Collaborative Approaches

Several existing frameworks illustrate the potential of multi-stakeholder collaboration:

• **ICZM**: This approach integrates stakeholders from various sectors to ensure sustainable coastal development and conservation.

• **Marine Spatial Planning (MSP)**: A participatory process that allocates marine and coastal resources among competing uses, balancing ecological, economic, and social priorities.

Challenges and Opportunities

Challenges in establishing collaborative frameworks include power imbalances, conflicting interests, and limited capacity for coordination. However, these can be addressed through:

• **Capacity Building**: Providing training for stakeholders to improve their understanding of coastal resilience and collaboration processes.

• **Conflict Resolution Mechanisms**: Establishing clear procedures for addressing disputes and fostering trust among stakeholders.

• **Technology Integration**: Using tools such as GIS, remote sensing, and online platforms to facilitate communication, data sharing, and decision-making.

Chapter 8: Financing Coastal Resilience

Financing coastal resilience is a critical challenge as the impacts of climate change intensify, threatening ecosystems, communities, and economies. Effective funding mechanisms are essential to implement restoration projects, build adaptive infrastructure, and promote nature-based solutions that enhance coastal resilience. However, the costs of these initiatives often exceed the resources available to local governments and stakeholders, creating a significant financing gap.

This chapter explores innovative financing approaches for coastal resilience, including public funding, private sector investments, and blended finance models. It examines the role of climate finance mechanisms such as the GCF, blue bonds, and PES in supporting coastal adaptation and mitigation efforts. Additionally, the chapter highlights the importance of prioritizing equity and inclusivity in financial frameworks to ensure that vulnerable communities benefit from resilience investments. By leveraging diverse funding sources and aligning financial strategies with global sustainability goals, stakeholders can address the pressing need for sustainable and scalable solutions to protect coastal systems and livelihoods.

Financial Mechanisms (Blue Bonds, Carbon Credits, Ecosystem Valuation)

Financing coastal resilience requires innovative and sustainable financial mechanisms to bridge the gap between available resources and the growing costs of adaptation and mitigation efforts. Mechanisms such as blue bonds, carbon credits, and ecosystem valuation have emerged as critical tools to support the implementation of coastal resilience initiatives. These approaches leverage market-based solutions, public-private partnerships, and the intrinsic value of natural ecosystems to generate funding while promoting environmental sustainability.

Blue Bonds

Blue bonds are a financial instrument specifically designed to support sustainable ocean and coastal projects. Modeled after green bonds, blue bonds raise capital for initiatives that enhance the resilience of marine and coastal ecosystems while addressing environmental, social, and economic challenges.

• **Structure and Function**:

Blue bonds are issued by governments, development banks, or private entities to fund projects such as mangrove restoration, sustainable fisheries management, and the creation of marine protected areas. Investors are repaid over time with interest, typically supported by government-backed guarantees or revenue generated from the funded projects.

• **Benefits**:

• Blue bonds attract private capital for public projects, reducing the financial burden on governments.

• They incentivize sustainable practices, such as reducing overfishing or restoring degraded coastal habitats.

• These bonds often include favorable terms, such as low-interest rates, making them accessible for developing nations.

• **Examples**:

The Seychelles issued the world's first sovereign blue bond in 2018, raising $15 million to support sustainable fisheries and marine conservation. This pioneering initiative demonstrated the potential of blue bonds to generate funding for coastal resilience.

Carbon Credits

Carbon credits are market-based instruments that incentivize the reduction or sequestration of greenhouse gas emissions. Blue carbon ecosystems, such as mangroves, salt marshes, and seagrass meadows, are increasingly recognized for their ability to sequester significant amounts of carbon, making them valuable assets in carbon markets.

• How They Work:

Carbon credits are generated by projects that reduce emissions or enhance carbon storage. For example, restoring a mangrove forest can generate credits based on the amount of carbon dioxide sequestered by the ecosystem. These credits are then sold to companies or governments looking to offset their emissions.

• Benefits:

• Provides a financial incentive for conserving and restoring blue carbon ecosystems.

• Encourages private sector investment in nature-based solutions.

• Aligns with global climate goals by reducing atmospheric carbon levels.

• Challenges:

Establishing robust monitoring, reporting, and verification (MRV) systems is essential to ensure the credibility of carbon credits. Additionally, carbon markets must address concerns about equity, ensuring that local communities benefit from revenue generated by these initiatives.

• **Examples**:

Projects such as the Mikoko Pamoja initiative in Kenya use carbon credits to fund mangrove restoration while supporting local livelihoods. This community-driven project generates revenue from carbon markets to invest in education, water supply, and conservation efforts.

Ecosystem Valuation

Ecosystem valuation assigns a monetary value to the services provided by coastal and marine ecosystems, such as carbon sequestration, flood protection, and biodiversity support. This approach helps quantify the economic benefits of preserving natural systems, making it easier to justify investments in their protection and restoration.

• **Methods of Valuation**:

• **Direct Market Value**: Based on the revenue generated by ecosystem-related goods, such as fisheries or tourism.

• **Avoided Costs**: Measures the savings from ecosystem services, such as the cost avoided by using mangroves for flood protection instead of constructing seawalls.

• **Willingness to Pay**: Surveys and studies estimate how much individuals or communities are willing to pay to preserve ecosystems or access their benefits.

• **Applications**:

Ecosystem valuation can inform cost-benefit analyses for coastal resilience projects, demonstrating the economic advantages of protecting natural habitats. For example, studies have shown that restoring mangroves often provides a return on investment by reducing the costs of flood damage and maintaining fisheries productivity.

• **Policy Integration**:

Valuation data can guide policy development, encouraging governments and businesses to prioritize ecosystem conservation. For instance, including ecosystem values in national accounting systems, such as Gross Domestic Product (GDP), highlights the contribution of natural capital to economic growth.

Synergies Between Mechanisms

Blue bonds, carbon credits, and ecosystem valuation are complementary mechanisms that can be integrated to enhance their impact:

• **Blue Carbon Projects**: Restoration projects funded by blue bonds can generate carbon credits, creating additional revenue streams.

• **Valuation for Investment**: Ecosystem valuation helps quantify the economic returns of resilience projects, attracting investors to blue bonds or carbon markets.

• **Policy Alignment**: By combining these mechanisms within a broader policy framework, stakeholders can promote sustainable coastal management while achieving financial and environmental goals.

Challenges and Considerations

Despite their potential, these financial mechanisms face several challenges:

• **High Initial Costs**: Developing projects that qualify for blue bonds or carbon credits often requires significant upfront investment.

• **Data and Monitoring Gaps**: Accurate data is critical for ecosystem valuation and carbon credit verification, but many regions lack the necessary resources for monitoring.

• **Equity Concerns**: Ensuring that local communities benefit from these mechanisms is essential to avoid marginalization and build long-term support.

Cost-Benefit Analysis of Blue Carbon Systems and Estuarine Restoration

Blue carbon systems, including mangroves, salt marshes, and seagrass meadows, and estuarine restoration efforts offer immense ecological, social, and economic benefits. These ecosystems play a critical role in carbon sequestration, coastal protection, biodiversity support, and providing resources for local communities. A cost-benefit analysis (CBA) of these systems highlights their long-term value, demonstrating that their restoration and conservation yield returns that far exceed initial investments. Despite some challenges in quantifying certain benefits, the overwhelming evidence supports their inclusion in sustainable coastal management strategies.

Costs of Blue Carbon Systems and Estuarine Restoration

Restoration and conservation efforts require significant upfront and ongoing investments. These costs are associated with the physical, technical, and social aspects of restoring and maintaining these ecosystems.

• **Restoration and Maintenance Costs**:

Replanting mangroves, restoring tidal flows, or stabilizing sediment in seagrass meadows involves labor, materials, and technical expertise. For example, mangrove restoration can cost between $100 and $1,000 per hectare, depending on the site's degradation level and the scale of the project.

• **Monitoring and Management**:

Continuous monitoring of restored ecosystems to ensure their success is a recurring expense. This includes employing advanced technologies like remote sensing or local surveys to track ecosystem health and carbon sequestration performance.

• **Opportunity Costs**:

Restoring blue carbon ecosystems often involves limiting or halting economic activities such as aquaculture, agriculture, or urban development, which can generate short-term losses for stakeholders.

Benefits of Blue Carbon Systems and Estuarine Restoration

The benefits of restoring blue carbon ecosystems and estuarine habitats are diverse, extending far beyond ecological gains. When quantified, these benefits illustrate the significant economic value of investing in restoration.

• **Carbon Sequestration and Climate Mitigation**:

Blue carbon ecosystems sequester and store large quantities of atmospheric carbon dioxide in their biomass and soils. Mangroves, for example, can store up to 1,000 metric tons of carbon per hectare. The financial value of this service can be estimated through carbon credits, which provide a market mechanism for monetizing carbon sequestration.

• **Coastal Protection**:

Mangroves and salt marshes act as natural barriers against storm surges, flooding, and erosion. Studies show that these ecosystems reduce wave energy by up to 60%, protecting infrastructure and reducing disaster recovery costs. The avoided costs from damages can significantly outweigh restoration investments.

• **Biodiversity and Fisheries**:

Restored estuaries and blue carbon systems provide critical habitats for marine species, supporting biodiversity and enhancing fisheries. These benefits translate into economic gains for local fishing industries and ecotourism opportunities.

• **Water Quality Improvement**:

Estuarine and blue carbon systems filter pollutants, sediments, and nutrients from water, improving water quality and reducing the need for costly human-engineered filtration systems.

• **Community Livelihoods and Well-Being**:

Coastal communities benefit from the ecosystem services provided by restored habitats, such as food security, employment in ecotourism, and increased resilience to climate impacts. These social benefits, though harder to quantify, are critical to local development.

Comparing Costs and Benefits

The CBA of blue carbon systems and estuarine restoration reveals that the long-term benefits often far exceed the initial costs.

• **Return on Investment (ROI)**:

Research indicates that every dollar invested in mangrove restoration can yield up to $10 in ecosystem service benefits over time.

Similarly, salt marsh and seagrass restoration projects demonstrate high ROIs through avoided damages, increased fisheries yields, and carbon market revenue.

• **Monetized Benefits**:

The financial benefits from carbon credits, disaster risk reduction, and fisheries alone often justify the costs of restoration. For example, a restored mangrove forest not only protects a coastal village from flooding but also generates revenue through carbon markets and ecotourism.

• **Non-Monetized Benefits**:

Many benefits, such as biodiversity conservation and cultural value, are difficult to assign a monetary value but contribute significantly to the overall success and sustainability of these systems.

Challenges in Cost-Benefit Analysis

While the evidence overwhelmingly supports the economic viability of blue carbon and estuarine restoration, several challenges complicate the analysis:

• **Data Limitations**:

Comprehensive data on carbon sequestration rates, ecosystem services, and long-term benefits are not always available, particularly in developing regions.

• **Valuing Non-Market Benefits**:

Assigning monetary value to benefits such as biodiversity, cultural significance, or community resilience remains complex and subjective.

• **Long-Term Perspective**:

Restoration projects require a long-term outlook to capture the full extent of their benefits, which can conflict with the short-term priorities of governments or investors.

Role of Public-Private Partnerships in Funding

Public-private partnerships (PPPs) play a crucial role in financing coastal resilience initiatives by leveraging the strengths and resources of both public and private sectors. These collaborations help bridge funding gaps, promote innovation, and ensure the sustainable implementation of projects. As the demand for adaptive solutions to climate change and coastal degradation grows, PPPs provide an effective mechanism for mobilizing investments and sharing responsibilities in addressing complex coastal challenges.

Understanding Public-Private Partnerships

PPPs are collaborative agreements between public entities, such as governments or international organizations, and private sector stakeholders, including corporations, financial institutions, and NGOs. These partnerships are structured to distribute the costs, risks, and benefits of projects in ways that align with the interests and expertise of each party.

• **Public Sector Contributions**:

Governments and public agencies typically provide regulatory support, access to land or natural resources, and partial funding. They also ensure alignment with policy objectives and facilitate community engagement.

• **Private Sector Contributions**:

Private entities contribute financial investments, technical expertise, and innovative solutions. Their involvement often accelerates project timelines and enhances efficiency in implementation.

Importance of PPPs in Coastal Resilience

PPPs are particularly valuable in coastal resilience projects, where the financial and technical demands often exceed the capacity of public institutions alone. Key benefits include:

• **Mobilizing Resources**:

PPPs attract private capital to fund large-scale coastal projects, such as mangrove restoration, flood control infrastructure, and hybrid solutions combining green and grey infrastructure. By reducing reliance on public budgets, these partnerships make it possible to undertake ambitious initiatives that would otherwise be infeasible.

• **Promoting Innovation**:

Private sector involvement introduces advanced technologies and innovative approaches, such AI, remote sensing, and sustainable engineering designs. These innovations enhance the effectiveness and scalability of coastal resilience measures.

• **Risk Sharing**:

PPPs distribute financial and operational risks between public and private partners. For example, private entities often assume the risks associated with project construction and maintenance, while public institutions provide long-term regulatory and policy support.

Examples of PPP Models

Several models of PPPs have been successfully applied in funding coastal resilience projects:

• Build-Operate-Transfer (BOT):

In this model, private entities finance and construct coastal infrastructure, such as storm surge barriers or wastewater treatment facilities. They operate the project for a defined period to recover costs and generate profit, after which ownership is transferred to the public sector.

• PES:

PPPs in PES schemes involve private entities funding the restoration or preservation of coastal ecosystems, such as mangroves or coral reefs, in exchange for the ecosystem services they provide, such as carbon sequestration or flood mitigation.

• Blue Bonds:

Governments and development banks collaborate with private investors to issue blue bonds, raising capital for coastal and marine conservation projects. The private sector benefits from returns on investment, while public entities ensure alignment with resilience objectives.

Challenges in PPP Implementation

Despite their potential, PPPs in coastal resilience face several challenges:

• Complex Coordination:

Aligning the interests and priorities of diverse stakeholders can be difficult, particularly when public goals such as community well-being conflict with private profit motives.

• **Regulatory and Policy Barriers**:

Inconsistent or unclear regulations can hinder the development and implementation of PPPs. For instance, delays in permitting or land-use approvals can stall projects and increase costs.

• **Ensuring Equity**:

PPPs must balance financial returns with social equity, ensuring that benefits, such as improved coastal protection or ecosystem restoration, reach vulnerable communities without creating additional financial burdens.

Opportunities for Scaling PPPs

To enhance the role of PPPs in funding coastal resilience, several strategies can be adopted:

• **Policy Support**:

Governments can create enabling environments for PPPs by streamlining regulations, providing incentives, and establishing clear frameworks for collaboration.

• **Innovative Financing Mechanisms**:

Combining PPPs with innovative tools, such as blended finance and impact investing, can attract a broader range of investors while ensuring social and environmental outcomes.

• **Community Involvement**:

Engaging local communities in PPP projects ensures that initiatives address local needs, build trust, and promote long-term sustainability.

Innovative Funding Strategies for Nature-Based Solutions and Technology

Funding the implementation of NBS and advanced technologies for coastal resilience requires innovative approaches to address financial constraints, engage diverse stakeholders, and ensure scalability. Traditional funding sources, such as government budgets or international aid, are often insufficient to meet the growing demand for adaptive and sustainable coastal management solutions. Innovative funding strategies are therefore critical to bridging this gap and unlocking new opportunities for investment.

Blended Finance

Blended finance combines public and private capital to de-risk investments in NBS and technologies. By leveraging public funds or philanthropic contributions to absorb initial risks, this approach encourages private investors to participate in projects that may otherwise seem too uncertain or unprofitable.

• **Structure**: Public entities provide guarantees, first-loss capital, or concessional loans, making the project more attractive to private investors.

• **Example**: Mangrove restoration projects funded through blended finance often use public funds to cover early-stage costs, such as site preparation, while private investors benefit from long-term returns through carbon credits or improved fisheries.

Green and Blue Bonds

Green bonds and their ocean-focused counterpart, blue bonds, are innovative tools for raising capital for sustainable projects. These debt instruments attract investors seeking environmental or social impact alongside financial returns.

• **Application**: Proceeds from blue bonds can fund coastal protection projects, such as coral reef restoration or hybrid infrastructure integrating mangroves and seawalls.

• **Example**: The Seychelles' sovereign blue bond has been instrumental in financing sustainable fisheries management and marine conservation, demonstrating how such instruments can support both NBS and community resilience.

Payment for Ecosystem Services

PES schemes reward landowners or communities for conserving ecosystems that provide critical services, such as carbon sequestration, water filtration, or flood protection. By monetizing these services, PES creates direct financial incentives for implementing NBS.

• **Mechanism**: Stakeholders, such as governments, NGOs, or private companies, pay for the measurable benefits derived from restored or protected ecosystems.

• **Example**: A PES program might compensate coastal communities for maintaining healthy mangrove forests that act as natural flood barriers, reducing the need for expensive engineered solutions.

Carbon Markets and Blue Carbon Credits

Carbon markets provide opportunities to finance NBS by generating revenue from the carbon sequestration potential of ecosystems like mangroves, seagrass meadows, and salt marshes.

• **How It Works**: Restoration or conservation projects quantify the carbon they sequester and sell the resulting carbon credits to corporations or governments seeking to offset emissions.

• **Example**: Blue carbon projects, such as Kenya's Mikoko Pamoja initiative, generate revenue through carbon credits while also delivering co-benefits like biodiversity support and improved livelihoods.

Crowdfunding and Community Investments

Digital platforms enable communities, individuals, and small investors to contribute to NBS and technology projects.

• **Approach**: Crowdfunding campaigns can raise funds for local resilience initiatives, such as the installation of flood sensors or the planting of mangroves.

• **Benefits**: This strategy not only provides funding but also fosters community involvement and ownership of projects.

Technology-Focused Venture Capital

Private venture capital is increasingly targeting technologies that address coastal challenges, such as AI-driven monitoring systems, drones for ecosystem assessment, and innovative engineering solutions.

• **Opportunities**: Early-stage investments in startups developing resilience technologies can drive innovation while generating financial returns.

• **Example**: Venture capital firms specializing in green technology fund projects that integrate cutting-edge tools with sustainable practices, such as hybrid NBS solutions.

Chapter 9: The Future of Coastal Resilience

The future of coastal resilience lies at the intersection of innovation, collaboration, and adaptability. As climate change accelerates and coastal communities face increasing threats from rising seas, extreme weather events, and ecosystem degradation, the need for transformative solutions becomes more urgent. The path forward requires integrating emerging technologies, scaling up nature-based solutions, and fostering inclusive, equitable governance frameworks.

This chapter explores the critical trends, opportunities, and challenges shaping the future of coastal resilience. It examines how advancements in science, technology, and policy can address the evolving needs of coastal systems, while highlighting the importance of community engagement and global collaboration. By embracing a forward-thinking approach, stakeholders can build resilient coastal regions that not only withstand climate impacts but also thrive in an uncertain future.

Emerging Trends in Blue Carbon and Sustainable Wetland Management

As the impacts of climate change intensify, blue carbon ecosystems and wetlands have emerged as critical components of climate mitigation and adaptation strategies. These systems, including mangroves, seagrass meadows, salt marshes, and coastal wetlands, offer unparalleled carbon sequestration capabilities while providing essential ecosystem services like flood protection, water purification, and biodiversity support. Recent advancements in science, policy, and technology are driving innovative approaches to blue carbon and wetland management, ensuring their sustainability and resilience in a rapidly changing world.

Advances in Blue Carbon Science

The growing recognition of blue carbon ecosystems as vital carbon sinks has spurred significant research and technological advancements, improving their integration into climate strategies.

• **Enhanced Carbon Measurement and Monitoring**:

Emerging tools such as remote sensing, drones, and satellite imagery are revolutionizing the ability to measure and monitor blue carbon stocks with precision. High-resolution data allows for more accurate quantification of carbon sequestration in mangroves, salt marshes, and seagrasses, supporting their inclusion in carbon accounting frameworks.

• **Blue Carbon Dynamics and Climate Resilience**:

Recent studies have highlighted the dynamic nature of blue carbon ecosystems and their resilience to climate impacts. For instance, mangroves have been shown to migrate inland in response to rising sea levels, while seagrasses adapt to changes in sedimentation and nutrient availability. Understanding these dynamics informs adaptive management strategies that enhance long-term carbon storage.

• **Role of Microbial Communities**:

Emerging research on microbial communities in wetland soils is shedding light on their role in enhancing carbon storage. These microbial processes influence the decomposition of organic matter and methane emissions, making them a critical area of study for maximizing carbon sequestration benefits.

Policy and Market Integration

Global and regional policy frameworks are increasingly incorporating blue carbon and wetland systems into climate action plans, while innovative market mechanisms provide financial incentives for their conservation and restoration.

- **Inclusion in NDCs**:

Many countries are now incorporating blue carbon ecosystems into their NDCs under the Paris Agreement. By recognizing their carbon sequestration potential, governments are aligning conservation efforts with climate goals, creating opportunities for funding and international collaboration.

- **Carbon Markets and Blue Carbon Credits**:

The establishment of blue carbon credits in voluntary and compliance carbon markets is gaining momentum. Projects that restore or protect blue carbon ecosystems can generate credits, which are sold to companies or governments seeking to offset their emissions. This market-based approach incentivizes investments in sustainable wetland management.

- **Ecosystem-Based Adaptation Policies**:

Policies promoting ecosystem-based adaptation (EbA) increasingly emphasize the importance of wetlands and blue carbon systems in mitigating climate risks. These policies support hybrid solutions, combining natural and engineered approaches for flood control and coastal protection.

Technology-Driven Innovations

Technology is playing a transformative role in advancing the management of blue carbon and wetland ecosystems, enabling more effective conservation, restoration, and monitoring.

- **AI and Machine Learning**:

AI-powered models analyze large datasets to predict trends in blue carbon dynamics, assess ecosystem health, and optimize restoration efforts. These tools provide actionable insights for decision-makers and practitioners.

• **Remote Sensing and GIS**:

Remote sensing technologies, combined with GIS, enable large-scale mapping of blue carbon ecosystems. These tools identify degradation hotspots, track restoration progress, and monitor carbon fluxes in real-time, making them indispensable for sustainable management.

• **Innovative Restoration Techniques**:

New restoration techniques, such as drone-assisted mangrove planting and bioengineered seagrass modules, are improving the efficiency and scalability of restoration projects. These approaches reduce labor costs while ensuring higher survival rates for planted vegetation.

Community-Centered Approaches

Sustainable management of blue carbon and wetland systems increasingly emphasizes the involvement of local communities, recognizing their critical role in conservation efforts.

• **Community-Led Restoration**:

Many restoration projects now prioritize community engagement, empowering local populations to lead planting, monitoring, and maintenance efforts. This approach not only enhances project outcomes but also builds local capacity and fosters long-term stewardship.

• **Traditional Ecological Knowledge (TEK)**:

Indigenous and local knowledge systems are gaining recognition for their value in managing wetlands and blue carbon ecosystems. TEK provides insights into sustainable resource use, historical ecosystem dynamics, and adaptive responses to environmental changes.

• **Economic Incentives and Livelihoods**:

Integrating economic benefits, such as ecotourism and sustainable fisheries, into blue carbon and wetland projects ensures that local communities derive tangible value. This alignment of environmental and economic goals promotes long-term project sustainability.

Addressing Climate Change Challenges

As climate change accelerates, emerging trends focus on ensuring the resilience and adaptability of blue carbon and wetland systems in the face of evolving threats.

• **Sea-Level Rise Adaptation**:

Efforts are underway to identify and protect migration corridors for blue carbon ecosystems, allowing them to adjust to rising sea levels. Adaptive management strategies, such as reintroducing sediment flow to support marsh elevation, enhance ecosystem resilience.

• **Mitigating Extreme Weather Impacts**:

Wetlands and blue carbon systems are increasingly integrated into disaster risk reduction strategies, reducing the impacts of storms, flooding, and erosion. Restoring these ecosystems enhances their ability to buffer extreme weather events and protect coastal communities.

• **Restoring Degraded Ecosystems**:

Large-scale restoration initiatives, supported by global frameworks like the UN Decade on Ecosystem Restoration, focus on reversing the degradation of wetlands and blue carbon ecosystems. These efforts prioritize biodiversity conservation alongside climate goals.

Challenges: Rising Seas, Biodiversity Loss, and Resource Constraints

Coastal systems face escalating challenges driven by climate change, human activities, and natural variability. Rising sea levels, biodiversity loss, and resource constraints represent some of the most significant threats to the resilience and sustainability of coastal ecosystems. These interconnected challenges jeopardize the health of ecosystems, the livelihoods of coastal communities, and the success of conservation and adaptation initiatives. Understanding these issues is critical to developing effective solutions and long-term strategies for coastal resilience.

Rising Sea Levels

Sea-level rise is one of the most pressing challenges for coastal areas, exacerbated by global warming and melting ice sheets. It poses severe risks to ecosystems, infrastructure, and human settlements.

• **Flooding and Inundation**:

Rising seas increase the frequency and severity of coastal flooding, threatening low-lying areas and eroding shorelines. Coastal ecosystems like mangroves, salt marshes, and seagrass meadows are particularly vulnerable, as prolonged inundation can disrupt their natural processes and lead to habitat loss.

• **Salinization of Soils and Water**:

Saltwater intrusion into freshwater systems affects agricultural lands and drinking water supplies, creating challenges for coastal communities that depend on these resources. It also impacts wetland ecosystems, altering their vegetation composition and reducing their productivity.

• **Ecosystem Migration and Loss**:

While some ecosystems, such as mangroves, can migrate inland in response to sea-level rise, this adaptation is often constrained by human development and natural barriers. As a result, many coastal habitats face the risk of being "squeezed" between rising seas and fixed infrastructure.

Biodiversity Loss

Coastal ecosystems are some of the most biodiverse regions on the planet, providing critical habitats for countless species. However, biodiversity loss in these areas is accelerating due to habitat destruction, pollution, and climate change.

• **Habitat Degradation and Fragmentation**:

Urbanization, agriculture, and aquaculture have led to the large-scale conversion of natural habitats into human-dominated landscapes. This fragmentation disrupts ecosystem connectivity, making it difficult for species to migrate, reproduce, and survive.

• **Climate Change Impacts**:

Rising temperatures, ocean acidification, and changing precipitation patterns are altering the conditions that coastal species depend on. For instance, coral reefs are experiencing widespread bleaching events, while migratory birds face shifts in their timing and availability of stopover habitats.

• **Invasive Species**:

The introduction of invasive species, often facilitated by global trade and climate shifts, further threatens native biodiversity. These species can outcompete local flora and fauna, disrupt food webs, and alter ecosystem functioning.

• **Loss of Keystone Species**:

The decline or extinction of keystone species, such as oysters in estuaries or mangroves in wetlands, has cascading effects on ecosystem health. These species play crucial roles in maintaining ecosystem structure and function, and their loss reduces resilience to environmental changes.

Resource Constraints

Limited financial, technical, and human resources pose significant barriers to addressing coastal challenges and implementing resilience strategies effectively.

• **Funding Gaps**:

Coastal resilience projects, such as wetland restoration, blue carbon initiatives, and flood control infrastructure, require substantial financial investment. Many governments and communities lack the resources to fund large-scale efforts, particularly in developing countries where coastal areas are often most vulnerable.

• **Technical Capacity**:

Implementing advanced technologies for monitoring, restoration, and adaptation requires specialized knowledge and expertise. In many regions, there is a lack of trained personnel and technical infrastructure to support such initiatives, limiting their effectiveness and scalability.

• **Data and Knowledge Deficits**:

Effective decision-making depends on robust scientific data and traditional knowledge. However, gaps in baseline data, monitoring, and long-term research hinder the ability to assess ecosystem health, track changes, and plan adaptive responses.

• **Competing Priorities**:

Resource constraints are exacerbated by competing priorities, such as economic development and infrastructure expansion. These pressures often lead to the prioritization of short-term gains over long-term sustainability, undermining coastal resilience efforts.

Interconnected Nature of Challenges

The challenges of rising seas, biodiversity loss, and resource constraints are deeply interconnected, amplifying their impacts on coastal systems.

• **Feedback Loops**:

For example, the loss of coastal vegetation due to sea-level rise reduces the ecosystem's ability to buffer against flooding, leading to further degradation. Similarly, biodiversity loss weakens ecosystem resilience, making it harder to recover from disturbances such as storms or pollution events.

• **Unequal Impacts**:

Vulnerable populations, particularly in developing countries and small island states, are disproportionately affected by these challenges. Limited resources and infrastructure exacerbate their vulnerability, highlighting the need for equity-focused solutions.

Addressing the Challenges

While these challenges are significant, addressing them requires targeted strategies and collaborative approaches:

• **NBS**:

Restoring and conserving blue carbon ecosystems, such as mangroves and salt marshes, can mitigate the effects of rising seas while enhancing biodiversity and carbon sequestration.

• **Innovative Funding Mechanisms**:

Tools like blue bonds, carbon credits, and PES can mobilize resources to address funding gaps and support resilience initiatives.

• **Technology and Data Integration**:

Leveraging remote sensing, AI, and community-based monitoring can improve the understanding of coastal dynamics and inform adaptive management.

• **Global and Local Collaboration**:

International frameworks, such as the Paris Agreement and the SDGs, alongside local community engagement, can drive coordinated action and build capacity to address these challenges.

Vision for Coastal Systems in 2050: Sustainability and Innovation

By 2050, coastal systems can become models of sustainability, innovation, and resilience, driven by a combination of technological advancements, nature-based solutions, and inclusive governance. As climate change continues to reshape the world, coastal regions will need to adapt dynamically while maintaining ecological balance, protecting communities, and fostering economic growth. The vision for coastal systems in 2050 centers on leveraging innovation and collaboration to ensure that these vital areas thrive in the face of challenges.

Sustainable and Resilient Ecosystems

In 2050, coastal ecosystems such as mangroves, coral reefs, and wetlands will serve as the foundation of resilience, restored and managed to optimize their ecological and socio-economic benefits.

• **Restored Blue Carbon Ecosystems**:

Restored and protected blue carbon ecosystems will play a critical role in mitigating climate change. Mangroves, salt marshes, and seagrass meadows will be widely recognized for their ability to sequester carbon while providing flood protection and supporting biodiversity.

• **Thriving Biodiversity**:

Coastal ecosystems will host robust biodiversity, with endangered species recovering due to effective conservation measures and habitat restoration. Fisheries will be sustainably managed, ensuring long-term food security and livelihoods for coastal communities.

• **EbA**:

Nature-based solutions will be central to coastal resilience strategies, combining ecological restoration with innovative engineering to address climate risks such as sea-level rise and extreme weather events.

Cutting-Edge Technological Integration

Technological innovation will be at the forefront of coastal management in 2050, enabling data-driven decision-making, efficient resource use, and enhanced protection of coastal systems.

• **Advanced Monitoring Systems**:

Real-time monitoring powered by AI, remote sensing, and autonomous drones will provide comprehensive insights into coastal dynamics. These systems will track shoreline changes, ecosystem health, and climate impacts, allowing for immediate action and adaptive management.

• **Predictive Modeling**:

Machine learning algorithms and big data analytics will predict future scenarios, such as storm surge impacts, erosion patterns, and biodiversity shifts. These tools will support proactive planning and risk reduction.

• **Smart Infrastructure**:

Hybrid green-grey infrastructure will integrate advanced materials and renewable energy technologies with natural systems, creating multi-functional structures that protect coastlines while supporting ecosystem services.

• **Blue Economy Innovation**:

Sustainable aquaculture, renewable energy from tidal and wave systems, and eco-tourism will thrive, driven by technological advancements that minimize environmental impact and maximize economic opportunities.

Inclusive and Collaborative Governance

In 2050, governance frameworks will prioritize inclusivity, equity, and global cooperation to ensure sustainable coastal management.

• Community Engagement:

Coastal communities will play a central role in decision-making, supported by participatory governance models that value traditional ecological knowledge and local expertise. Citizen science initiatives will empower individuals to contribute to monitoring and restoration efforts.

• Equity and Social Justice:

Governance systems will address historical inequities, ensuring that marginalized and vulnerable populations benefit from coastal resilience investments. Resources will be allocated fairly, with targeted support for low-income and climate-vulnerable regions.

• Global Collaboration:

International agreements and regional partnerships will strengthen, aligning efforts to combat shared challenges such as sea-level rise, pollution, and overfishing. Collaborative funding mechanisms, such as the Green Climate Fund, will ensure sustained financial support for coastal resilience initiatives.

Climate Adaptation and Mitigation

Coastal systems in 2050 will embody integrated approaches to climate adaptation and mitigation, balancing ecological, social, and economic priorities.

• Dynamic Adaptation Strategies:

Coastal regions will implement flexible and adaptive strategies to respond to changing conditions. Managed retreat, wetland migration corridors, and flood-resilient urban planning will minimize risks and protect communities.

• **Carbon Neutrality**:

Coastal ecosystems will contribute significantly to global carbon neutrality goals, supported by robust blue carbon markets and incentives for ecosystem preservation. Restoration projects will generate carbon credits, attracting investment from corporations and governments.

• **Disaster Risk Reduction**:

Resilient coastal systems will reduce the impacts of extreme weather events through natural defenses, reducing reliance on hard infrastructure and lowering disaster recovery costs.

Education and Capacity Building

Education and capacity building will be cornerstones of sustainable coastal management, fostering awareness, innovation, and long-term stewardship.

• **Education Programs**:

Environmental education programs will be integrated into schools and communities, promoting awareness of coastal resilience and sustainability. These programs will inspire future generations to become advocates and innovators in coastal conservation.

• **Research and Innovation Hubs**:

Coastal regions will host research hubs dedicated to developing cutting-edge solutions for resilience and sustainability. Collaboration between scientists, policymakers, and local stakeholders will drive innovation.

• **Capacity Building for All Stakeholders**:

Governments, communities, and private-sector actors will benefit from training programs that build technical and governance capacities, ensuring effective and equitable management of coastal systems.

Call to Action for Collaboration and Long-Term Planning

Achieving coastal resilience in the face of escalating climate challenges requires collaboration, long-term vision, and proactive planning. Coastal ecosystems are dynamic, interdependent, and critical for the well-being of both people and the planet. As such, no single stakeholder, organization, or sector can address the complexities of coastal management alone. A unified effort is essential to protect these vital systems, ensure sustainable livelihoods, and safeguard the future for generations to come.

Strengthen Collaboration Across Stakeholders

Collaboration must extend across all levels of governance, sectors, and communities to ensure holistic and inclusive solutions. Governments, international organizations, private businesses, academic institutions, and local communities each have a role to play.

• **Governments and Policymakers**: Develop and implement integrated policies that prioritize coastal resilience, drawing on input from all stakeholders.

• **Private Sector**: Invest in innovative technologies, nature-based solutions, and sustainable practices that contribute to resilience while supporting economic growth.

• **Communities**: Engage in decision-making processes and stewardship efforts, sharing traditional knowledge and supporting localized solutions.

• **Global Collaboration**: Strengthen international agreements and partnerships to address shared challenges, such as sea-level rise, pollution, and habitat degradation.

Commit to Long-Term Vision and Planning

The dynamic nature of coastal systems demands long-term strategies that are flexible, adaptive, and forward-thinking. Proactive planning is essential to mitigate risks, protect ecosystems, and ensure sustainable development.

• **Climate Adaptation**: Integrate nature-based solutions with innovative technologies to address the impacts of sea-level rise, extreme weather, and ecosystem loss.

• **Equitable Policies**: Prioritize vulnerable and marginalized populations in resilience planning, ensuring fair distribution of resources and benefits.

• **Future-Proofing**: Anticipate future challenges and opportunities by investing in research, education, and capacity-building programs that empower stakeholders to act effectively.

Act Now for a Resilient Future

The time to act is now. Delays in addressing the challenges facing coastal systems will lead to greater costs, risks, and irreversible damage. Collaborative action today will create lasting benefits for ecosystems, economies, and communities.

Conclusion

Coastal systems are at the forefront of the global fight against climate change, biodiversity loss, and rising sea levels. These ecosystems provide invaluable services, including carbon sequestration, coastal protection, and support for biodiversity and livelihoods. Yet, they face unprecedented threats from human activities and environmental changes. The need for sustainable and innovative approaches to coastal resilience has never been more urgent.

This book has explored the critical components of coastal resilience, focusing on blue carbon ecosystems, estuarine buffers, sustainable wetland management, technological advancements, and governance frameworks. Together, these elements form the foundation for addressing current challenges and building adaptive, resilient coastal systems for the future. The integration of NBS and advanced technologies offers a powerful pathway for mitigating climate risks while preserving ecosystem functions and services.

Achieving coastal resilience requires a shift in how stakeholders perceive and manage coastal ecosystems. The traditional reliance on engineered solutions is no longer sufficient in the face of dynamic and complex coastal challenges. Instead, a balanced approach that combines natural and technological solutions is necessary to address the interconnected social, economic, and environmental dimensions of coastal resilience. Blue carbon ecosystems, for example, are vital carbon sinks and natural barriers against storm surges, but their potential can only be fully realized with robust monitoring and management systems supported by advanced technologies.

Governance and policy frameworks must also evolve to ensure inclusivity, equity, and long-term sustainability. Collaborative governance models that engage local communities, governments, private sector actors, and international organizations are essential for developing effective strategies. Coastal resilience is not just about protecting ecosystems—it is about ensuring the well-being of the millions of people who depend on these systems for food, water, shelter, and livelihoods. Equitable policies that prioritize vulnerable populations and promote community engagement will be critical to achieving inclusive resilience.

The future of coastal resilience depends on proactive planning and innovative funding mechanisms. Tools such as blue bonds, carbon credits, and blended finance can mobilize resources to support large-scale restoration and conservation projects. Public-private partnerships and global collaborations are also key to unlocking investments and scaling up resilience initiatives. By aligning financial strategies with sustainability goals, stakeholders can ensure that resources are directed toward impactful, long-term solutions.

Looking ahead, the vision for coastal systems in 2050 is one of sustainability, innovation, and inclusivity. These systems have the potential to become thriving, adaptive landscapes that balance ecological integrity with human needs. Realizing this vision will require continued advancements in science and technology, coupled with strong governance and community involvement. It will also require a shared commitment to preserving and restoring coastal ecosystems as essential allies in combating climate change and supporting global sustainability goals.

The path forward is clear: we must act collectively and decisively to protect coastal ecosystems and communities from the growing threats they face. By embracing integrated approaches, fostering collaboration, and prioritizing long-term planning, we can build a resilient future for coastal systems. The time to act is now, and the opportunity to create lasting change is within our reach. Together, we can ensure that these vital systems continue to thrive, providing benefits for both people and the planet for generations to come.